A STORY

200 YEARS of METHODISM in BRIGHTON and HOVE

by Michael R. Hickman
Circuit Archivist

Maps by
Shirley Veater

A history of Methodism in Brighton and Hove to celebrate the bicentenary of the creation of the first Methodist circuit in the city.

All profits from the sale of this book will go the
Brighton and Hove Methodist circuit

Published by Brighton and Hove Methodist circuit
Stanford Avenue Methodist Church
Stanford Avenue, Brighton, BN1 6FD

ISBN 978 0 9556506 0 4

© Copyright: Michael R. Hickman, September, 2007

All rights reserved.
No part of this book may be reproduced, stored in a any retrieval system, or transmitted, in any form or by any means, electronic, mechanical photocopying or otherwise without the permission of the publishers.

printed in Great Britain by
One Digital
54 Hollingdean Road
Brighton, BN2 4AA

TABLE of CONTENTS

Foreword		1
Introduction		3
Chapter 1	Methodism - Foundations	8
Chapter 2	Brighton	19
Chapter 3	The Early Years 1807-1860	28
Chapter 4	Expansion and Union 1860-1934	44
Chapter 5	From Union Onwards 1934-2007	58
Chapter 6	Buildings and Finance 1807-2007	66
Chapter 7	The Spiritual Life of the Church I	84
Chapter 8	The Spiritual Life of the Church II	96
Chapter 9	The Church and its Young People	106
Chapter 10	Leadership in the Church	114
Chapter 11	Life in the Church	126
Chapter 12	The Church in the Wider Society	133
Chapter 13	Conclusion	145

Maps of Brighton and Hove

Methodist Churches in 1860	26-27
Methodist Churches in 1934	42-43
Methodist Churches in 2007	56-57

FOREWORD

One of my maxims is that 'history can be a good teacher but a poor companion'. The story contained in this book, thoughtfully written by the author, is a good example of what I believe to be true. In the pages that follow there is overwhelming evidence of careful research and a passion for the subject: always the mark of the historian. At the same time there is also an awareness of what we might learn from our forebears with the warning not to look at the past through 'too many rose-coloured spectacles'. These pages illustrate the challenges and struggles of our ancestors in the faith. For the truth is that each generation has to contextualise the faith in a way that is relevant and appropriate and as these pages show that has never been an easy task.

The Brighton and Hove circuit owes a great debt of gratitude to Michael Hickman for chronicling its story so as to encourage us in the current task of 'serving the present age'. It has been a true labour of love and a memorable way to help the Brighton and Hove circuit celebrate 200 years of Methodism.

The Rev. Kathleen Allen
Superintendent minister
Brighton and Hove circuit
July 2007

Charles and John Wesley

(Methodist Recorder Photograph)

INTRODUCTION

In the nineteenth century the area of England lying between London and the south coast, especially the counties of Surrey and Sussex, was thought of as the 'Methodist Wilderness', but not all was quite as bleak as might be thought from that description.

Although the first Methodist prayer meeting was held in Brighton 1804 and a Methodist 'class meeting' established soon after that it is with the creation of a new circuit in September, 1807 that Methodism was securely founded in Brighton and Hove and it is that bicentenary that we are celebrating in 2007 (the technical terms will be explained later).

This book is written as part of the celebration of that 200th anniversary of the first Methodist circuit in Brighton and Hove and must be read in that light. From Methodist union (achieved in Brighton and Hove in 1934) until 1997 there were two circuits in Brighton and Hove: the Brighton (Dome Mission) circuit and the Brighton & Hove circuit. In 1997 these combined to form the Brighton and Hove circuit. The ampersand has been used in this book to distinguish between the Brighton & Hove circuit(1934-1997) and the Brighton and Hove circuit(1997 to the present).

What is written here builds on the work and achievement of others. In 1923 the Rev. Lewis Court wrote, *'These Hundred Years'*, a history of the Bible Christian (from 1907 the United Methodist) churches in Brighton and Hove, together with the story of the brief existence of the United Methodist Free Church. In 1957, to celebrate the 150th anniversary of the first circuit, the Rev. Ernest Griffin wrote, *'A Pilgrim People'*, giving the history of all branches of the Methodist family in the area to that date.

The late archivist of the Brighton & Hove circuit, James Antony (Tony) Funnell, was indefatigable in his researches and wrote brief histories of almost all the Primitive Methodist Churches in Brighton and Hove, together with a booklet on the most well-known Primitive Methodist minister, the Rev. William Dinnick. He also wrote histories of the Bristol Road Bible Christian Church and of Hollingbury Methodist Church. I am very grateful indeed to his widow, Doreen Funnell, for passing on to me his extensive collection of notes, newspaper cuttings and photographs.

In addition Hove Methodist Church (the Rev. Colin Smith and Peter Nurcombe, 1996), Patcham Methodist Church (Nanette Buck, 1995), and Stanford Avenue Methodist Church (Marjorie and Harold Cozens, 1998) have each had their story written.

W. T. Thorns produced an early account of the Dome Mission in 1946, *'Fishing for Men'* and its sixtieth anniversary was recounted by Norman Moody in 1967, *'Sixty years at the Dome 1907-1967'*. In 1985, as an edition of the Dome Mission Magazine, *Outreach,* Len Wright, my predecessor as archivist of the Brighton (Dome Mission) circuit, produced a history of Dorset Gardens Methodist Church and the Dome Mission to celebrate the centenary of the opening of the new building at Dorset Gardens. David Rutter kept a wonderful series of scrapbooks of the Dome Mission from 1975 until 1993.

There are a few other very useful works on local Methodism. In the early 1880s J. Sawyer wrote a series of detailed newspaper articles on many of the churches in Brighton. These were collected and published in book form in c. 1882 under the title: *'The Churches of Brighton - Descriptive Sketches of their Past History & Present Circumstances, with outlines of Sermons'*. This collection includes two churches in the Methodist family that followed the teaching of the Wesleys: Bristol Road Bible Christian Church and Dorset Gardens Wesleyan Methodist Church.

Some unpublished these have proved helpful. *'The Origins and Development of the Methodist Sunday School in*

19th Century Sussex' 'The Origins and Development of the Methodist Sunday School in 19th Century Sussex' in 2004 by Jacqueline Brown, and *'Methodism in Sussex and its influence in the life of the community 1756-1900'* in 1984 by Rowland Smith.

My very grateful thanks go to two libraries and record depositories. First, to Anna Manthorpe and all her colleagues at the East Sussex County Record Office who have helped my researches over so many years. One of the papers at the Record Office is a manuscript history of the Wesleyan Methodists in the nineteenth century written by one or more members of the Beves family, which has proved very helpful for the early period.

Secondly, to Peter Forsaith, the librarian/archivist of the Wesley Historical Society Library in the Wesley Centre, Oxford, Westminster Institute of Education, Oxford Brookes University who has never ceased to be of help.

I would also like to thank Drew University, New Jersey, U.S.A.; Duke University, North Carolina, U.S.A.; Englesea Brook Chapel & Museum; and the Society of Cirplanologists for letting me have copies of the few extant Preaching Plans for Brighton and Hove from before 1910.

I am very grateful to all of those who have helped with the photographs, many of which have suffered the ravages of age: to Doreen Funnell for the collection of the late James Antony (Tony) Funnell, Jonathan Gravestock, Paul Harrington. Susan Hickman and *The Methodist Recorder*.

The maps have been thoughtfully created by Shirley Veater to whom very many thanks are due.

Without the labours and enthusiasm of all of these, and the assistance of so many more, this book could never have been produced.

In writing an account of different Methodist traditions over two hundred years a number of questions arise. The first concerns anachronisms. All Methodist ministers are now termed 'the Rev.' or 'the Revd.' This style started in Wesleyan Methodism in 1811 so it does not apply to the earliest Wesleyan ministers here. Bible Christian and Primitive Methodist ministers used this style much later, and some not at all. The very word 'minister' was not used by all. Ministers sent to circuits by their respective Conference were first known as 'travelling Preachers', or 'Preachers of the Gospel'. Bible Christian ministers might well be called 'pastor' instead of 'minister'.

Sometimes the same word meant different things in different branches of Methodism. For most Methodists the word 'Superintendent' refers to the minister in charge of a circuit. But Bible Christians used 'Superintendent' for the minister who was the equivalent in other Connexions of the Chairman of a District. I have used such terms as they would have been applied by most within the Methodist tradition.

To avoid confusion I have decided to use 'the Rev.' and 'minister' throughout aware that the early ministers might well have felt affronted by such usage.

For most of Methodist history the buildings for worship have been called 'chapels', they still are in some cases. In Brighton and Hove they are all now called 'churches' and I have used that word here.

In order to try to differentiate between the different groups before Methodist union in 1932 I have used the word Connexion with a capital to indicate the whole group called Wesleyan Methodist or Bible Christian. The word 'Church' is used for the Methodist Church or for a specific building, e.g. Woodingdean Church.

The word or phrase used for what is now often called the Eucharist has also changed over the years. The words 'sacrament', 'Lord's Supper', 'Communion', have all been used by Methodists both locally and nationally. The *Methodist Worship Book* published in 1999 uses 'Holy Communion'. Where the noun is needed I have used 'Holy Communion' where the adjective is required I have used 'eucharistic'. The current Methodist hymn book is *Hymns & Psalms (H&P)* and will be referred to by those initials. Other Methodist terminology will be explained as it arises.

All the Connexions in Brighton and Hove had churches in other parts of Sussex in their circuits at various times. This book deals almost exclusively with those in the area of the modern city of Brighton and Hove.

Methodists, like other groups, do not live in time capsules unaffected by cultural, religious, political and aesthetic developments. If they did they would find themselves, like time capsules, buried to be dug up by later generations curious to discover what this long-gone group did. Therefore reference has to be made to developments in church thinking and activity on a wider scale than that of this city and I have tried to tell the story of the 'people called Methodist' in Brighton and Hove with some regard to the local, national, and even international context. It is difficult otherwise to understand why events occur as they do.

Much though some Methodists might regret it, Methodism in all its forms, has moved on from the days of John Wesley although in certain aspects, for example regular communion, contemporary Methodists may be said to have recaptured their founder's ideas better than their nineteenth century forbears. The story of how they have changed and developed in Brighton and Hove over these two hundred years will now be told.

CHAPTER 1

METHODISM

FOUNDATIONS

In the 1720s and 1730s a religious revival began in many parts of north America and northern Europe including Britain. The movement in Britain gave rise to two strands that were both called 'Methodist' at the time. Each was founded by clergymen of the Church of England with the aim of spreading a 'pure' Christianity throughout the land and of giving renewed life to the Church of England. One of these clergymen, George Whitefield (1714-1770), on his return in 1739 from the first of his seven visits to America, found that many Anglican clergy refused to allow him to preach in their Churches so, following the example of the Welsh preachers Griffiths Jones (1683-1761) and Howell Harris (1714-1773), he began to preach in the open-air, attracting huge crowds. Some thought that this activity was both dangerous and irregular, if not illegal, but Whitefield and his friends discovered that it was a very successful way of bringing their message to many thousands untouched by the normal life of the Church of England and they continued to preach wherever they could.

Two of Whitefield's clergyman friends were the brothers John (1703-1791) and Charles Wesley (1707-1788). They followed Whitefield's example and also began to preach in the streets and fields. All preached with passion and fervour, emphasising God's love and the necessity of a personal experience of salvation. They travelled around the country spreading this message and John Wesley himself covered an estimated 250,000 miles and preached about 40,000 sermons until his death in 1791.

Whitefield was supported strongly by a number of wealthy people amongst whom the most prominent was Selina, Countess of Huntingdon (1707-1791). She came 'to Brighton in 1755 hoping that the sea and air of the place would be beneficial to the health of her ailing youngest (sic) son.' Whitefield preached for her here and she built in North Street the first of what became a number of churches of 'the Countess of Huntingdon's Connexion', enlarging it in 1767.

It was possibly because Whitefield had made Brighton one of his mission fields that neither John nor Charles Wesley visited the town, a fact commented on by all writers on the history of Methodism in Brighton. However, John Wesley had intended to join Whitefield there on at least one occasion, writing in 1767 from Liverpool about his regret at not being able to join him, and the fact that the second of the Countess of Huntingdon's churches was built at Bath had not stopped the Wesleys from visiting that town on many occasions.

Although they were friends there were some major differences between Whitefield and the Wesleys. The most important of these concerned who could be saved. Whitefield followed the majority view of the Reformation and of seventeenth century England and held that God had chosen only some people to be saved. This view is known either as 'Calvinist' after the reformer John Calvin (1509-1564) or 'predestination' because God was believed to have chosen people's eternal destiny before they were born.

The Wesleys took a different view. They held that God wanted all people to be saved. This view was known at the time as 'Arminian' after the Dutch theologian, Jacobus Arminius (1560-1609). Charles Wesley was a great hymn-writer and his hymns expressed the brothers' beliefs very well indeed. Indeed it is said that if you want to know what Methodists believe, look at their hymn book: Methodists sing their theology.

For example, two of Charles Wesley's early hymns, written in 1742, have these lines:

> *"Thy sovereign grace to all extends,*
> *Immense and unconfined;*
> *From age to age it never ends;*
> *It reaches all mankind."* (H&P 46 v 2)

and

> *"For all my Lord was crucified,*
> *For all, for all my Saviour died."* (H&P 226 v 7)

These lines with their emphasis on 'all', could never have been written by a Calvinist. Until the death of Whitefield in 1770 these differences were generally kept at bay by their mutual friendship and respect and John Wesley preached the sermon at Whitefield's memorial service in London. However, the difference, which was profound, continued to grow and the magazine that John Wesley started in 1778 was called the 'Arminian Magazine', with its first article on the life of Arminius, in order to emphasise the rejection of Calvinism by the Wesleys.

This difference was felt strongly by the early Methodists in Brighton one of whom wrote: '… Calvinism of the highest type was taught from various pulpits in the neighbourhood and there were none to apply the Scriptural Antidote to this objectionable teaching.' This feeling persisted amongst the Methodists who followed the Wesleys. A leading Primitive Methodist speaking at a Congress of Methodists in 1929 listed the evils of the eighteenth century and placed 'Calvinism' between 'illiteracy' and 'limited franchise'.

Consequently it is no surprise that the first Methodist church in Brighton, built in Dorset Gardens in 1808, was registered in the name of the 'Arminian Methodists' and called at first 'the Arminian Chapel'. This must have been done in order to distinguish it from the church of the Countess of Huntingdon's Connexion in North Street.

> certify to your Lordship that a certain Chapel lately erected in Dorset Gardens St James's Street in the Parish of Brighthelmstone in the County of Sussex is intended to be used for Religious Worship by a Congregation of Protestant Dissenters denominated Arminian Methodists. And we do hereby desire that the same may be registered in your Lordship's Registry pursuant to the Directions of an Act of Parliament made in the first Year of the Reign of their late Majesties King William and Queen Mary entitled 'An Act for exempting their Majesties' Protestant Subjects dissenting from the Church of England from the Penalties of certain Laws' As Witness our Hands this twenty fifth Day of August 1808 – Robert Pilter – Minister. – Saml. Akehurst. – Richard Robarts. – William Mitchell – Edwd Beves – John Pocock. –

Extract from the registration of Dorset Gardens as place of worship for the 'Arminian Methodists'. It is signed 25 August, 1808 by Robert Pilter and Richard Robarts, the ministers, and Samuel Akehurst, William Mitchell, Edward Beves and John Pocock. The document was only rediscovered in the Dorset Gardens Church safe in 2003.

From now on the word Methodist will be used solely in relation to the family of Connexions that followed the tradition founded by John and Charles Wesley.

One of the hallmarks of Methodism was its organisation. The Wesleys and their supporters preached, converted and organised those converted before moving on. It was this organisational ability, exemplified in the activity of John Wesley, that enabled the movement that the Wesley brothers founded to grow and develop and survive John Wesley's death in 1791 by which point it had over 70,000 members.

When someone became a member of a Methodist society he or she was placed in a class. This class met each week under a leader to discuss the state of their souls and to develop their spiritual growth. At first each town had a 'society'. Gradually as the movement grew so places like Bristol, London and Newcastle, the three corners of John Wesley's usual triangle of travelling, had more than one society in different parts of the city or town. Methodists were encouraged to attend their parish church and to take communion regularly. This latter practice was unusual in the eighteenth century in which taking communion four times as year, or just once, was more usual. However, the Wesleys believed that taking communion was a 'means of grace' and wanted their followers to emulate their own example of regular communion.

John Wesley found that he and his fellow Church of England clergymen were far too few to visit all the societies that he founded so he accepted the necessity of allowing some of his lay followers, including women, to preach. He appointed a number of these preachers to travel around a large number of societies which were eventually grouped together in circuits. Starting in 1744 he invited some travelling preachers to join him and his few fellow clergymen in an annual conference to discuss matters of importance. As the numbers in the societies grew so the number of circuits increased and these were grouped together in districts. For their mutual convenience there were regular meetings of representatives of each of societies, circuits and districts. The leaders of the local societies and circuits were appointed by the travelling preachers (also called 'itinerant preachers') and were called stewards.

Whilst there have been many changes over the years this basic pattern has been followed by all the major groups who have been part of the Methodist family. As the terms here will be used throughout this book it might be helpful to list them here. As mentioned in the introduction not all Methodists used the terms in exactly the same way, in addition the functions of the original meeting, such as the Quarterly Meeting, may well be different from its successor, the Circuit Meeting: but it will serve as a useful guide.

TERMS USED in METHODISM

CLASS — Led by **CLASS LEADER** (now called a **PASTORAL VISITOR**). Most Methodists no longer 'meet in class' but the terminology is often still used.

SOCIETY — A number of classes led by **SOCIETY STEWARDS** (now called **CHURCH STEWARDS**). The Class Leaders and the Society Stewards met regularly in the **LEADERS' MEETING** (now called the **CHURCH COUNCIL**). Societies also appointed **POOR STEWARDS** (now called **COMMUNION STEWARDS**) whose original function was to help the poor members of the societies.

CHAPEL — A society usually built or bought a chapel for itself. This meant that a society was effectively synonymous with a particular place of worship. The building itself was under the control of **TRUSTEES** until 1976 when the Trusts disappeared and their role was taken over the by the newly formed Church Councils. The Trustees appointed **CHAPEL STEWARDS** (now called **PROPERTY STEWARDS**) to look after the property on a regular basis. Gradually Chapels became known as Churches. At times there was conflict between the Trustees and the Society.

CIRCUIT The grouping of societies in a local area. The Society Stewards together with the Poor Stewards, the Trustees and the preachers who only preached in that circuit, called **LOCAL PREACHERS**, met with the travelling preachers, the **MINISTERS,** once a quarter. This was known as the **QUARTERLY MEETING** (now called the **CIRCUIT MEETING**). Ministers were appointed to the circuit, not to the local Society. The senior minister was called the **SUPERINTENDENT**. One of the roles of the Superintendent minister was to decide who was going to preach in each chapel at each service. This was called making the **PLAN**.

DISTRICT Once or twice a year the ministers and leading laity in each circuit of a District met together in a **SYNOD**.

CONFERENCE Representatives from the Districts and the circuits met annually. For most Methodists the Conference was the decision-making body and held ultimate responsibility.

CONNEXION To quote from the *Dictionary of Methodism in Britain and Ireland*:

'[The] connexional principle continues to be intrinsic to Methodism, as a structural expression at all levels of church life of essential interdependence, through fellowship, consultation, government and oversight.'

It is a feature of Methodism that they feel themselves interconnected.

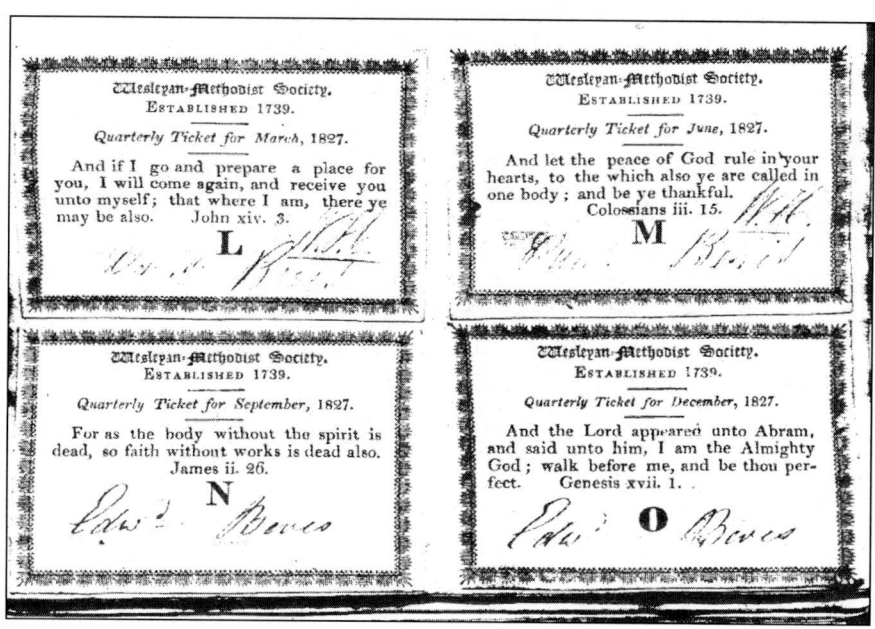

The Wesleyan Methodist Class Tickets of Edward Beves (son of Edward Beves, founder of Methodism in Brighton) for the four quarters in 1827

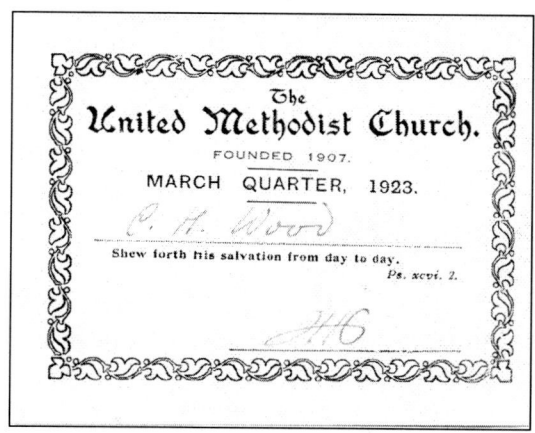

The United Methodist (ex-Bible Christian) Class Ticket for C. H. Wood for March Quarter, 1923

DIVISIONS WITHIN METHODISM

After John Wesley's death in 1791 government of the Methodist societies was in the hands of the annual conference of ministers, hardly any of whom were ordained clergymen of the Church of England. By 1794 Methodism had effectively become a separate Church from the Church of England. Over the next sixty years there were a number of divisions from the main body, called the Wesleyan Methodists. We will refer here mainly to those which affect Brighton and Hove.

In the first two decades of the nineteenth century there were further revivalist movements that started within Wesleyan Methodism but the leaders of these movements were expelled from it. This was the period of the Napoleonic wars and the unrest that followed it and the legal position of Wesleyan Methodism was not clear for some time. Consequently Wesleyan Methodism was keen to avoid all provocation of the government and disliked anything 'irregular'. In the Potteries and in the west country two such irregular movements began independently and gathered strength. That in the Potteries, the Primitive Methodists, became the second largest Methodist Connexion after the Wesleyans. That in the west country, the Bible Christians, remained a comparatively small group with few members outside Devon and Cornwall. Both connexions eventually had churches in Brighton and Hove.

There were also groups who broke away from the parent Wesleyan body. Until 1878 the Wesleyan Conference consisted of ministers only and tended to be dominated by a few leading ministers of whom the most important was the Rev. Jabez Bunting (1779-1858). A number of people increasingly resented Bunting's long dominance of Wesleyan Methodism. There had already been some breakaways from the Wesleyans but in 1828 there was a dispute in Leeds between the trustees and the society over whether to have an organ in a church, and in 1834-1835 there was a disagreement over the establishment of a ministerial training college, with Bunting at its head. The tension between what was perceived to be the ministerial authority of the 'pastoral office' and the growing confidence and independence of the laity continued.

During the 1840s a series of anonymous pamphlets called the *'Fly Sheets'* were circulated amongst the ministry. These were attacks, of 'vigorous invective', on the leadership of Wesleyan Methodism, especially on Bunting. At the 1849 Conference the leadership tried to discover the authorship of the *Fly Sheets.* The result was that three ministers were expelled from Wesleyan Methodism, effectively because they would not answer the question of authorship. *The Times* called their expulsion: 'a threat to the liberty of the Press' and called the Conference: 'an irresponsible tyranny'.

The furore aroused deep passions over the ministerial monopoly of Conference and during the next few years over 100,000 members left or were expelled from Wesleyan Methodism. In the years 1850 and 1851 Wesleyan Methodism lost over 55,000 members, either resigning or expelled, more that 15% of its total membership. Many, but by no means all, of those who left, eventually formed the United Methodist Free Church in 1857. Although the disruption had a great impact in Brighton and Hove the United Methodist Free Church itself had only a brief existence in the area.

One of the major differences between the Wesleyan and other Methodist groups was the role given to the laity. As we have seen, until 1878 the Wesleyan Methodist Conference consisted only of ministers. The Bible Christian Conference had an equal number of ministers and lay representatives and the Primitive Methodist Conference had a ratio of two laymen to one minister. Although both the Primitive Methodists and the Bible Christians had women ministers in their early years they each gradually moved to an all-male ministry. The

Wesleyan Methodists had an all-male ministry throughout the nineteenth century.

Whilst all groups of Methodists appealed in the nineteenth century to the 'skilled worker', called 'artisans': the Wesleyan Methodists had a greater strength among shopkeepers and the Primitive Methodists a greater strength amongst the miners and agricultural and other labourers. Primitive Methodism was also strong amongst the railway workers in places like Didcot and Swindon. The Bible Christians had a similar social profile to the Primitive Methodists but were far more rural.

The 'Dissenters' of the eighteenth century were those groups who had 'dissented' from the ideas of the Church of England. 'Old Dissent' consisted of the Baptists, Independents and Presbyterians, together with the Quakers. The Wesleys always thought of themselves as members of the Church of England and had disliked being linked with 'Old Dissent'. However, during the nineteenth century all Methodist Connexions, the Wesleyans last of all, considered themselves more and more as part of the dissenting tradition. Methodism formed part of what is called 'New Dissent' and, together with 'Old Dissent', the words 'Nonconformist' or 'Free Church' began to be applied to all of these groups.

The overall impact of the movements claiming descent from the Wesleys was great. By 1851, the occasion of the only religious census in England and Wales before 2001, the total number of those who attended worship in churches of the Methodist tradition was only just less than half of those recorded for the Church of England and was greater than any other nonconformist group.

CHAPTER 2

BRIGHTON

It is a common misconception that Brighton's fame as a seaside resort and its consequent growth stemmed from the Prince Regent's visits when Prince of Wales and his building of the Royal Pavilion. Before the Prince of Wales paid his first visit in 1783, Brighton was already the largest seaside resort in the country. One of its advantages was its proximity to London, only a day's journey on the coach.

However, the arrival of the Prince Regent and his decision to build what became the Royal Pavilion clearly had a major impact on the development of the town. In addition Brighton was also a major military base during the wars with France between 1792 and 1815. All of this meant that Brighton grew rapidly, being one of the fastest growing towns in the country between 1801 and 1811 and the fastest growing town of all between 1811 and 1821.

In 1801 there were very few churches in Brighton. The Church of England had the parish church of St. Nicholas which was joined by the Chapel Royal in 1793 as a 'chapel-of-ease'. In addition there was the church built by the Countess of Huntingdon, a new Quaker Meeting House in Ship Street, just opened in 1800 replacing a earlier building, and the Union Chapel, built by dissenters in 1683.

As most of the churches were enlarged between 1801 and 1851 the total number of available seats in 1801 must have been less than the 4,500 recorded for these buildings in 1851. With a population of 7339 in 1801 the majority could not have attended church on Sunday even if they had wanted to.

NAME of CHURCH	BUILT	NUMBER of SEATS in 1851	ALTERATIONS
St. Nicholas	medieval	1410	
Chapel Royal	1795	800	
Countess of Huntingdon, North Street	1760	973	Enlarged in 1810 and 1822
Union Street Chapel	c. 1698	900	Much altered in 1822
Quaker Meeting House – now under New Road and Royal Pavilion	c. 1700	500	Moved to Ship Street in 1805. The figure refers to Ship Street
TOTAL		**4573**	

William IV, who became king in 1830, continued to use the Royal Pavilion but Queen Victoria, who came to the throne in 1837, found that it lacked privacy and did not return to the town after her last stay in 1845 save for the usual brief visits that she made to many places in the country.

This decline in royal patronage had little impact on the growth and development of Brighton. The railway had arrived in 1840 and the London-Brighton line was completed by September, 1841. This, with the advent of the excursion train and the day-tripper, changed Brighton into the 'modern seaside resort'. Consequently much, if not most, of the employment in the town was related to tourism in one way or another. In addition people began to commute to work and to retire to the area. The fact that there were 150 private schools in the town in the 1880s shows how popular a place Brighton had become, especially as it was considered to be a good place to send invalid children for the sake of their health.

The appearance of prosperity disguised the reality of life for many in Brighton. The *New Monthly Magazine* in 1841 described Brighton as a place of two distinct classes, 'those who make the town an hotel, and those who live by providing for their entertainment.' The dwellings of the poor were very bad indeed. As the *Encyclopedia of Brighton* notes: 'the slums were as bad as any to be found in London or the Industrial North ...'. In 1848 Dr. Kebbell, physician to the Brighton Dispensary, drew attention to this in a series of lectures. He pointed out that the sewer running through Edward Street was higher than the basement floor of the houses. The worst areas were the streets near Edward Street, like Dorset Street and Paradise Street. This was confirmed in an official report in 1849 which drew attention to the diseases caused by appalling conditions prevalent in these areas. This state of affairs continued for some time and the police could only patrol Edward Street in pairs in the 1860s because of the violence and drunkenness. In 1860 the number of shops engaged solely in the sale of alcoholic drinks was 479. By comparison the total number of bakers, butchers, grocers, fishmongers, greengrocers, etc. was 541. Slum clearance began in the 1870s and gradually the problems caused by overcrowding and insanitary conditions eased.

There were large numbers of working people in Brighton, but there was no major industry, although in 1891 the railway employees numbered over 2,600. This development of the railways was to have an impact on the growth of the Primitive Methodists in the town.

Hove, which was the adjacent parish to Brighton on its western side, grew far more slowly than Brighton and at times there were suggestions that it should be a part of Brighton. However, it survived on its own and grew only uniting with Brighton to become a unitary authority in 1997.

From the start of the twentieth century both Brighton and Hove began to expand into the Downs and absorbed some of the neighbouring ancient parishes such as Preston and Patcham. These areas became the suburbs and as the population moved to live there so the various branches of

Methodism followed them building churches in these new developments. Writing in 2007 it is interesting to note that of the six Methodist churches only two, Dorset Gardens and Stanford Avenue, are named after the roads in which they are situated: the other four, Hollingbury, Hove, Patcham and Woodingdean, are named after the areas that they serve.

It is necessary to appreciate this background in order to understanding the development of Methodism in the town. The earliest Wesleyan, Bible Christian and Primitive Methodist chapels were built in the streets off Edward Street, the poorest part of Brighton; although Dorset Gardens itself was quite a wealthy enclave with over half the households living there in 1851 having at least one living-in servant. It was not until the large railway community developed in Brighton in the last quarter of the nineteenth century that the Primitive Methodists were able to expand.

The five places of Christian worship in 1801 had increased by 1851 to 38 together with one synagogue. This expansion would continue throughout the rest of the century and the main role in the expansion was played by the Church of England which built a further fourteen churches, excluding school and hospital chapels, by 1901. This feature of Brighton's religious life is a mirror of the national picture for, as the social historian A. D. Gilbert noted: 'a higher proportion of the English population practised Anglicanism in 1914 than in 1830 …'

However Anglicanism in Brighton took a particular expression. Many of the churches, such as St. Bartholomew's, were built by followers of the Tractarian movement of the 1830s (also called the 'Oxford Movement' because it began in Oxford University). This movement within the Church of England came to be known as the Anglo-Catholic wing. It emphasised the authority of the Church and the Church of England's roots in the primitive Church and the 'Catholic' tradition. By the middle of the nineteenth century it was moving towards a high sense of ritual and ceremony, and was attacked by its opponents for its 'ritualism', or 'sacerdotalism'. An article written in 'Southern History' in 1983 was entitled, *"'Bells and Smells': London, Brighton and South Coast religion'*.

The Rev. H. M. Wagner was the Vicar of Brighton from 1824 until his death in 1870. He was immensely wealthy, and built a new church in Brighton, St. Paul's, for his son, the Rev. A. D. Wagner who was a follower of the Oxford movement. St. Paul's from the first was one of the most extreme of the ritualist churches in England. A. D. Wagner built three other such churches in Brighton, the most famous being St. Bartholomew's which was opened in 1874 and sited near the railway works. One of the main functions of these churches was to attract the poor.

Some members of the Church of England objected very strongly indeed to this movement, seeing it as a way in which the Roman Catholic Church was attempting to infiltrate the Church of England and great passions were aroused. Brighton was the scene of much conflict, including riots in 1867 outside St. James Proprietary chapel, St. James's Street where the priest, John Purchas, who owned the chapel, introduced ritual.

This is not the place for a history of the Oxford Movement but we need to understand the fear that it aroused for many in the Protestant tradition who equated the movement with Roman Catholicism and all that the memory of persecution under Mary I, the Spanish Armada, James II, etc. evoked. In Brighton the growth of the catholic wing of the Church of England was a 'burning issue'. In 1900 the general election in Brighton was contested between candidates of the Conservative party and John Kensit, the well-known Protestant agitator, who stood as an 'Independent Protestant' candidate. Kensit obtained 24.5% of the vote, almost exactly the same percentage as that of the Liberal candidate in the 1895 election.

As we shall see this aspect of Anglicanism had a great affect on the attitude and development of the various branches of Methodism in the area and contributed to the fact that, combined with the 'leisure' aspect, Brighton and Hove were always regarded as very difficult places for Methodists to work in. The 'difficulty' of Brighton was acknowledged by contemporaries. For example an article in the (Wesleyan) *Methodist Recorder* on 25 April, 1907 referred to the problems of 'wealth and fashion'. The United Methodist (previously Bible Christian) minister, the Rev. Lewis Court in his history of his Connexion in the area wrote in 1923 that Methodists admitted that the environment of 'London-by-the-Sea' had never been 'too congenial … for their cause'. This was echoed by the Primitive Methodist superintendent, the Rev. J. M. Gunson who, in a speech in 1930 on leaving the circuit after four years, stated that Brighton was: 'The hardest pitch upon which I have ever worked'. He cannot have been the only one. One of the more dismal statistics is that of the 71 Primitive Methodist ministers serving in Brighton and Hove between 1842 and 1890, 24 left the ministry, ten of these immediately after or during their ministry in Brighton!

For all that, different groups of Methodists did establish a foothold and with hard work and good leadership grew and developed and became an integral part of the community of Brighton and Hove.

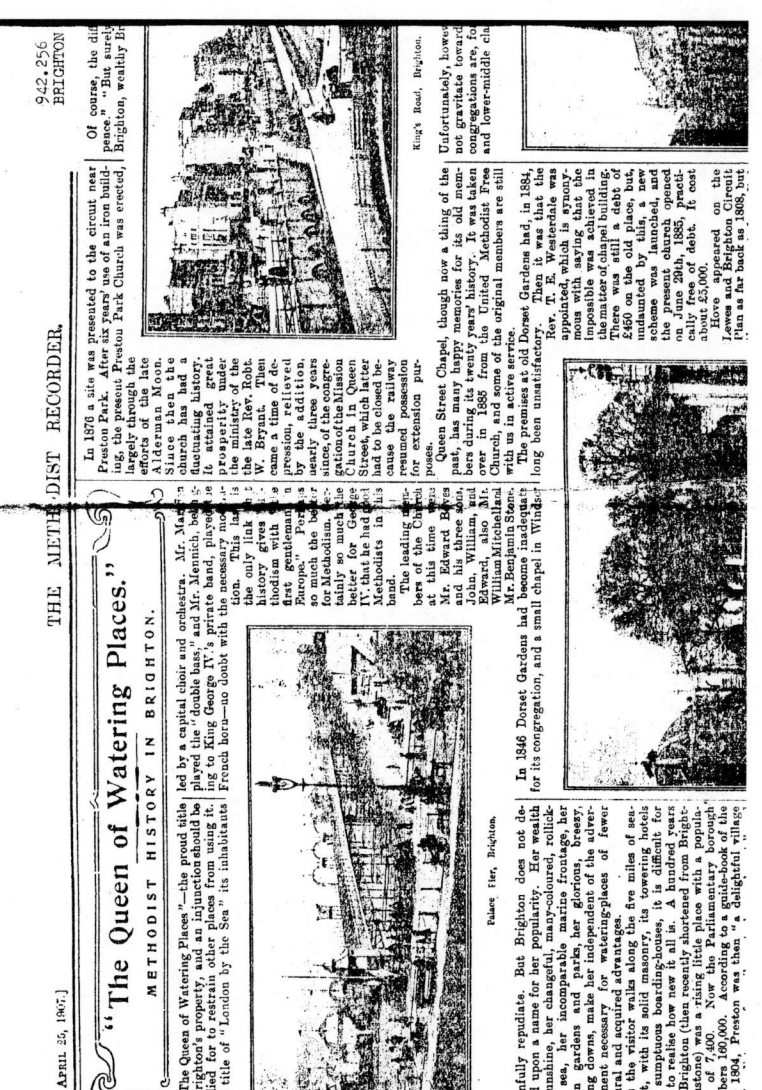

A page from the Methodist Recorder, 25 April, 1907 entitled "The Queen of Watering Places" Methodist History in Brighton
From the Library of the Wesley Historical Society.

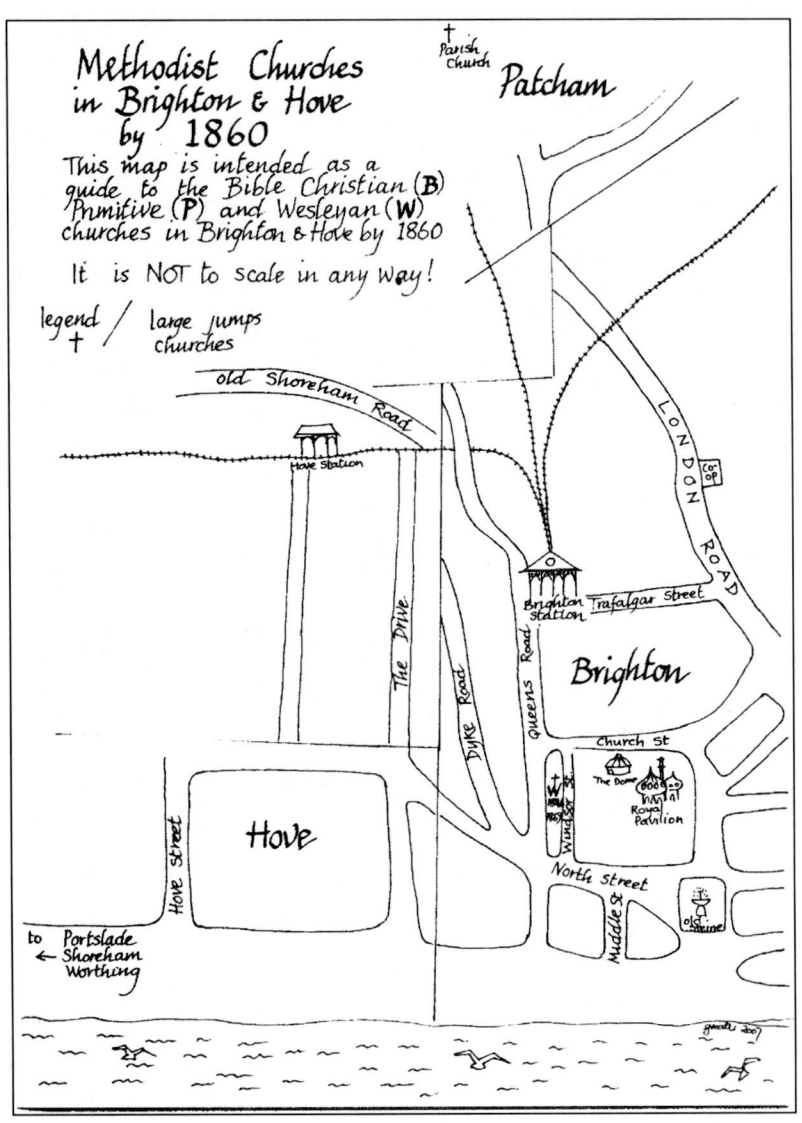

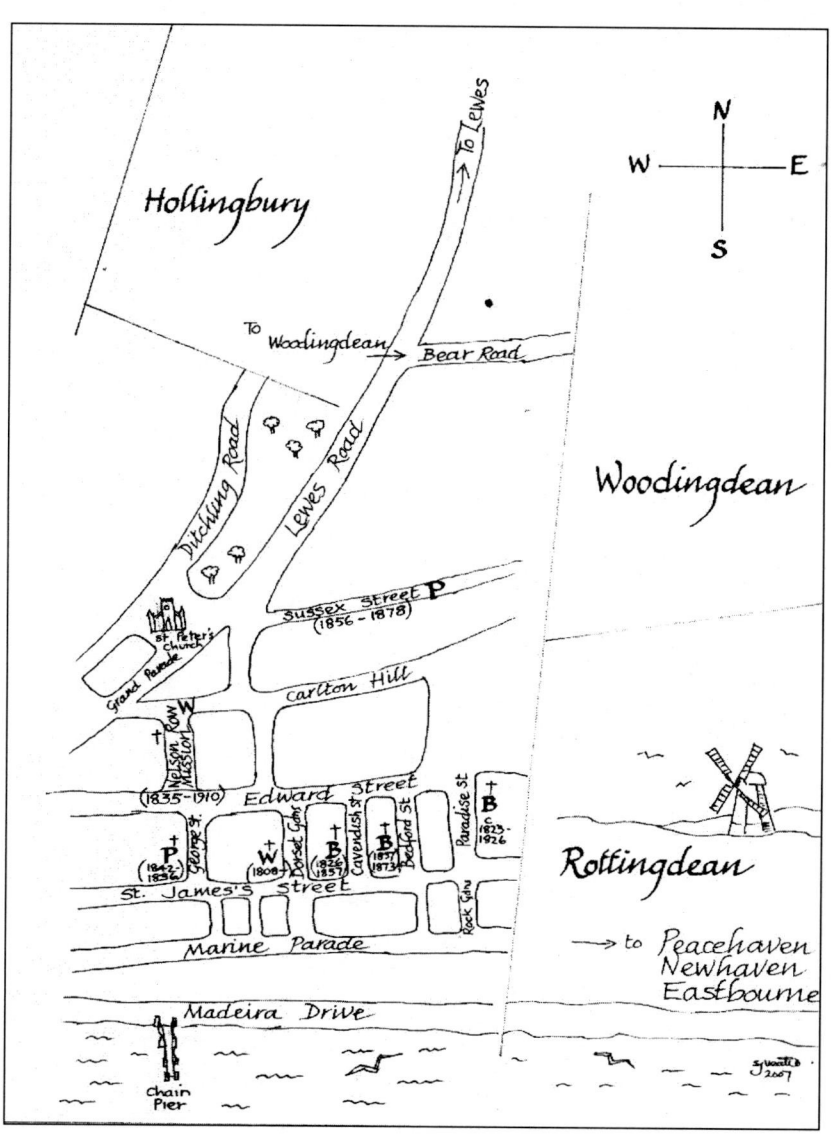

CHAPTER 3

The EARLY YEARS – 1807-1860

The WESLEYAN METHODISTS

The rapid growth of Brighton in the first decades of the nineteenth century led to much building and the first two Methodists to arrive, Edward Beves and William Mitchell, were carpenters. In a town growing so rapidly the skills of a carpenter would have been much in demand, the first Royal Pavilion was 'built principally of wood'. The most common occupation given for fathers in the local Wesleyan baptismal registers to 1837 is 'carpenter'.

The first to arrive was Edward Beves who came in the latter part of the eighteenth century from a strong Methodist family in Fareham. He looked for a place of worship and, according to the manuscript history of Wesleyan Methodism in nineteenth century Brighton: 'tried two or three nonconformist chapels' but they preached 'high Calvinist doctrine' so he worshipped instead at the local parish Church, St. Nicholas.

William Mitchell arrived from Northampton via London in the autumn of 1804. On his arrival he 'began to enquire for the Methodists but was bitterly disappointed to find there were none in the town.' At first he worshipped at the chapel of the Countess of Huntingdon's Connexion in North Street and from there formed a prayer group at his lodgings in Bond Street which was 'a great success [as] it was a new thing in the town & a number of young men and young women attended it (among the rest the young woman who afterwards became his wife)'. However the chapel leaders 'discovered that he was Methodist' and closed the prayer meeting. At some point soon after this he was employed by Edward Beves and the two remained firm friends, but there was still no Methodist society. This situation changed with the coming of soldiers.

In 1802 Britain had signed a Peace Treaty with Napoleon but it was generally regarded as being temporary and troops were moved to the south coast in 1804 and 1805 to counter the threat of invasion. Many of these troops were militia raised under the Militia Act of 1803, in addition thousands had volunteered their services. In the history of Methodism in Sussex this movement of soldiers to the south coast proved to be the turning point. Littlehampton, Lewes, Eastbourne, and Brighton each had regiments stationed in or near them which included a number of Methodists. It was this group that really started the Methodist societies in these towns.

The militia regiments stationed at Brighton included the 'North Yorks' and the 'South Gloucestershire'. These were both strong Methodist areas and some soldiers had 'established a prayer meeting in a cottage close to the barracks', and both Edward Beves and William Mitchell went to see them. They joined the prayer meeting and these visits were reciprocated by the soldiers and their wives.

A Methodist society of nine was formed from five Brighton families, including Edward Beves and his wife and William Mitchell and his wife, (William Mitchell married Eliza Williams, 26 December, 1804, so the first class meeting must be after that date). There was one other married couple, John and Sarah Pocock, Sarah, like William Mitchell, had worshipped at the Countess of Huntingdon's chapel, we do not know about John. They were soon joined by Samuel Akehurst and his wife, most of whose children to this point had been baptised at the Countess of Huntingdon's chapel.

So the first society can be seen as a group which had tried and rejected the Countess of Huntingdon's Church where Calvinism was taught.

The society met first at the house of one of its members, a Mrs Smith of 2 Middle Street, and then at the Pococks' house, also in Middle Street. The first meetings for congregational worship were held in a room in yet another house in Middle Street. This was a:

> 'long room or loft ... in a Yard in Middle S^t which had been used as a Dancing Room and tho by no means all that could be desired was the best that offered all was therefore secured'. It was Situate up a passage in the rear of 31 Middle S^t & had to be reached by a flight of wooden steps Pigs Goats & fowls were Kept by the occupant of the Yard'.

At its founding the society was placed in the Sevenoaks circuit, as were Eastbourne and Lewes. In 1807 the Conference established a new circuit, called 'Lewes and Brighthelmstone' with the Rev. Robert Pilter and the Rev. William Homer (styled 'Missionary') as ministers. Pilter was 23 years old and had been at Canterbury the previous year as a preacher 'on trial'. He was only 'admitted to full connexion', in other words accepted as a minister, at the 1807 Conference. He is therefore not only the first, but also the youngest and least experienced, of all the ministers of whatever branch of Methodism, to have been Superintendent here. Homer was in his first year of his three-year probationary period. It was a youthful leadership.

The circuit had ten societies and covered most of Sussex from Littlehampton to Robertsbridge and from Brighton to Tunbridge Wells. According to one of its early ministers, the Rev. Richard Robarts, it was: 'sixty miles long and thirty miles broad'.

The ministers and society in Brighton, although small (33 members in 1809), regarded their work with a missionary zeal and tried to establish other societies in the area: at Hove in 1809, Patcham in 1810, at Preston in 1823. In addition a preaching place at the Level, a large area of open ground on the northern borders of the parish of Brighton appears on the earliest surviving Wesleyan preaching plan, April-August, 1823.

The Rev. Robert Pilter, Wesleyan Methodist minister.
The first Superintendent minister in Brighton and Hove, 1807-1809.

However, all these early ventures failed and in 1823 the *Wesleyan Methodist Magazine* in describing the opening of an extension to Dorset Gardens commented that 'for several years the congregations were small, the Society few in number, and their discouragements many.'

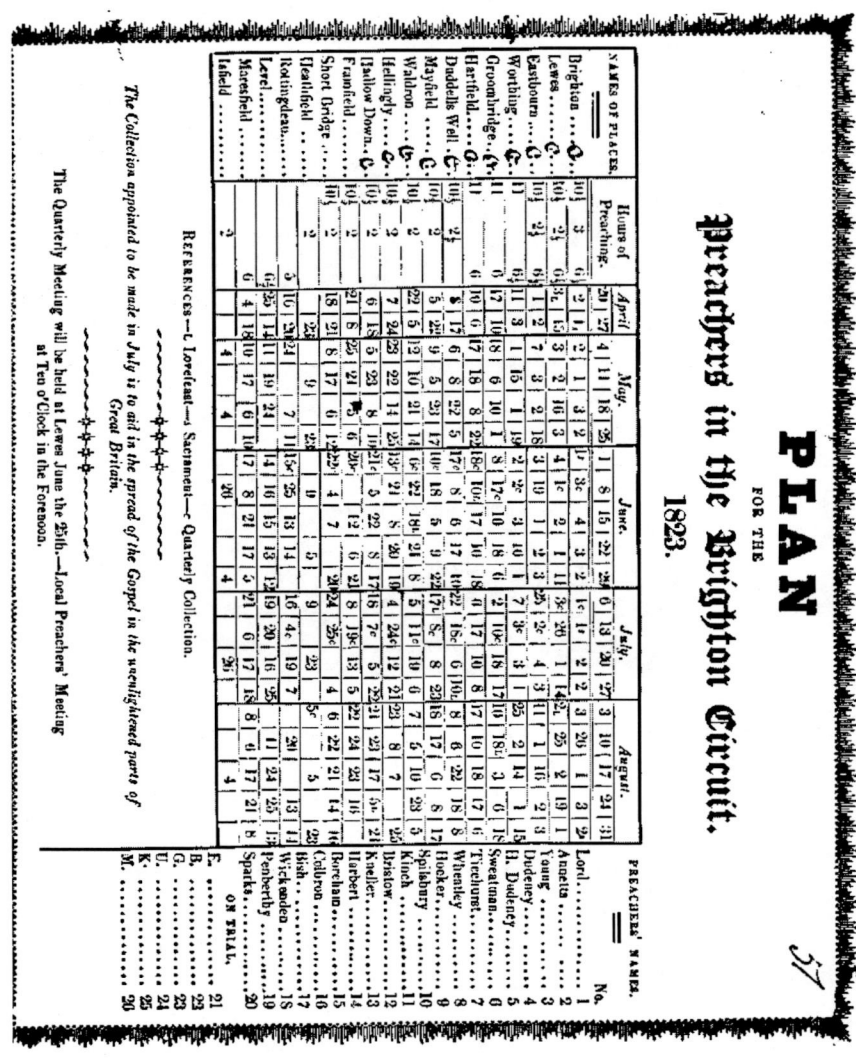

The earliest surviving Preaching Plan
April – August, 1823.

Reproduced with permission from the Thomas Marriott British Methodist Circuit Plans Collection, Drew University, USA

Despite these setbacks the Wesleyans persevered. The average number of Wesleyan baptisms each year of people living in Brighton from 1807 to 1822 was just over 7.5 per year. This rose threefold over the next fifteen years to an average of just over 24 per year. The Wesleyans extended their main church, Dorset Gardens, both in 1823 and in 1827 and, by splitting the circuit into two in 1825, creating one based on Brighton and the other on Lewes, were able to focus their efforts more effectively.

The baptismal registers recorded parental occupation for most baptism in years 1818-1837. Brighton Wesleyanism at this time was not a shop-keeping community, it was based on artisans with the biggest group of all, almost 14% of the 209 known families, being those described as 'carpenter', whereas only two of these families were 'grocers', and there were no drapers. Over the next hundred years this situation would change greatly.

The new Brighton circuit consisted of societies in Brighton and Worthing together with a very small one at Rottingdean. Shoreham soon appeared and Horsham was added in 1829 only to leave in 1833 to be replaced by a new society at Hurstpierpoint in 1833. Horsham was part of the Brighton circuit again in 1836 leaving in 1841 to become the head of its own circuit. We should not surprised at these changes. All Methodist connexions spread by the continual creation of societies and new circuits.

There were occasional setbacks. In 1834, the same year as one of the disruptions mentioned earlier, three class leaders and 19 other members left to join the Irvingites, a millenarian group that had started in 1833 in London. In 1851 its only place of worship in Sussex was in Grand Parade, Brighton.

Despite this the society at Dorset Gardens, still the only one in Brighton and Hove, continued to grow reaching 400 members by 1846. The population of Brighton was extending westwards and, to cater for this, a decision was taken in 1846 to rent a small chapel in Windsor Street, near the Clock Tower. This was meant to be a temporary expedient but financial pressures on the circuit meant that it was not until over twenty years later that the idea of building a chapel in western Brighton was put into effect.

Another reason for this delay must have been the impact of the great disruption within Wesleyan Methodism following the 1849 Conference which has been referred to in chapter 1.

Brighton was not immune from these troubles. It so happened that the minister appointed by that Conference to the Superintendency in Brighton in 1849 was the Rev. William Barton, a strong supporter of the leadership. This led to some angry feeling in the town. One of the trustees of the Sunday School, William Iles, was reported in 1850 as having an Anniversary advert in his shop window with Barton's name cut out. He was asked to change this but refused. He further refused to answer any questions at the Sunday School Committee and was censured.

The impact of this disruption in Brighton can be seen in that in June 1851 there were 334 members but by September of that year there were only 279, a loss of over 16%, very much in line with what happened nationally. By 1857 the number was even lower, only 267 members. However, unlike much of the rest of the country no separate congregation was formed at this time. It would not be until the 1880s that Wesleyan Methodism in Brighton recovered.

The UNITED METHODIST FREE CHURCH

In 1860 there was a further local disagreement and a meeting was called to form a new society separate from the Wesleyan Methodists. This was done and the Society joined the United Methodist Free Church which appointed a minister from 1862.

In 1867 this Society leased land from the railway company and built a church on the corner of Ann Street and Queen Street, near to the station. It became known as the Queen Street chapel. Of the ten trustees who lived in Brighton, no fewer than seven had jobs, such as 'engineer', that indicate a connection with the railway.

6, Queen Street.

Queen Street UMFC Church, from a photograph taken after it had been taken over by the Wesleyan Methodists in 1885 and before 1904.

The Society did not prosper and by 1885 it had disintegrated and the chapel passed to the Wesleyans who maintained a mission there. There are almost no records of this Society and we do not know why it failed. It may be that the vigorous work of the Primitive Methodists under the Rev. William Dinnick, who also appealed to the railway community, took away some of the members. They may also have lost members to the Salvation Army which arrived in Sussex in the early 1880s.

The BIBLE CHRISTIANS

The Rev. W. (Billy) Bailey, Bible Christian minister in Brighton 1825-1826

The Bible Christians were a west country group. Some people from Devon had gone to work in the dockyards at Chatham and were the basis of the Bible Christian community there in the early 1820s. From Chatham a few Bible Christians went to live in Brighton in 1823. In addition there were people like the Cornishman James Piper who had served for sixteen years in the army and then settled in Brighton. In 1824 missionaries from Chatham were invited. Famously two of the first were women, Ann Mason and Sarah Willis, who preached both in a rented room and in the streets. The *Brighton Herald* reported, with some surprise, that, 'tolerably correct language' was used and that their 'connections were respectable'.

The Rev. James Way, Bible Christian minister in Brighton, 1831-1832

From Brighton the ministers and others preached at places like Lewes and Wadhurst which had small societies by June 1825. However, they found it very difficult work. The Bible Christian appeal was to a rural constituency, especially people farming small areas of land. Brighton was hardly that area and the non-Anglican smallholders of east Sussex were mainly followers of different forms of Calvinist churches.

In 1827 it was decided to separate Brighton and Lewes from the societies in northern Sussex and make it into a circuit. By the 1851 census the early societies in east Sussex had disappeared and only the Brighton Society survived east of Arundel. As Court comments: 'For quite half a century the struggle for existence continued, and on various occasions the closing of the Mission was seriously considered'. Most ministers served for one year only, and it was not until 1857 that one minister, the Rev. James Barnden, served for three years. Of the 28 ministers who served before 1860 and whose birthplace is known, 75% came from small villages in Devon or Cornwall. Many of them must have found Brighton both surprising and perturbing. In 1842 the Rev. William Hopper wrote of his deep distress at what he found and how 'morning after morning, I have thrown myself on the floor to beseech God to have mercy on them.' Hopper came from Bradworthy in rural Devon on the border with Cornwall and had probably never been east of Devon before. Life in Brighton must have an immense shock for him. However, he went on to have a successful ministry and became President of the Bible Christian Conference in 1862.

At first the Society in Brighton worshipped in a variety of rooms and then moved to the singularly misnamed Paradise Street, between Hereford Street and Edward Street and now demolished, one of the poorest parts of Brighton. From there they moved in 1826 to Cavendish Street, very close to Dorset Gardens.

The Bible Christians remained in Cavendish Street, falling from 99 members in 1826 to 53 ten years later. From then onwards the average membership was about 40. A Conference Missionary deputation visited Brighton in 1843 and found 'things dull and the people greatly depressed by the lack of employment and the hard times which then obtained. In 1847 the Sunday School lapsed for 'want of suitable workers' and the minister in 1857 reported that 'the languishing state of the cause had been such for years that Conference had hesitated about continuing the labours of the preachers there.'

However, the Society still had hope and the Bible Christian Conference was willing to support them. In 1857 they bought a place of worship in Upper Bedford Street, close to the current Roman Catholic Primary School, which had been a privately owned Independent chapel.

For the first few decades of their existence in Brighton, therefore, the Bible Christians struggled to maintain a foothold. Their membership was undoubtedly poor and much affected by seasonal employment and periods of unemployment. Of the 26 families having children baptised between 1824 and 1837, ten described the father's occupation as 'labourer': there were also five 'shoemakers' and four 'carpenters'. Only one family had a slightly higher status, a 'corn dealer'. Of these 26 families, three, all 'shoemakers' had had their older children baptised at Dorset Gardens Wesleyan Methodist Church: one of these three families would eventually have children baptised by the Primitive Methodists.

The PRIMITIVE METHODISTS

The Primitive Methodists were the last group to arrive in Brighton. Some people in Brighton invited the Rev. William Harland, then missioning in the Isle of Wight and Portsmouth to come to them. This he did in 1836, walking from Portsmouth to Brighton in order to save money. A small society was established and in 1842 the Primitive Methodist Conference appointed its first minister. In 1851 the Society in Brighton rented a room in George Street, the road next to Dorset Gardens where the Wesleyan Church was. The following year they bought a site in Sussex Street but could not build a chapel there until 1856 for lack of funds.

Like the other Methodist connexions they missioned other areas and had societies in Shoreham and Lewes. As has already been mentioned the Primitive Methodists had their greatest success nationally amongst close-knit communities such as, the miners of the north-east, the agricultural villages of East Anglia, and the railway workers of the Great Western. The situation in Sussex was no different. By 1860 the society in Brighton was outnumbered by that in Shoreham, and one reason can be seen from an analysis of the occupations of families having their children baptised at this time. Excluding the ministers, of the 36 families in Brighton, seven were 'labourers' and the rest had a variety of occupations, with only three shopkeepers. The list does however include one wine-cooper!

In Shoreham however, of the 32 families having children baptised, eighteen had fathers described either as 'mariners' or 'sailors', five of these eventually described themselves as 'master mariners'. Clearly the Primitive Methodist message had an appeal to the maritime community in Shoreham.

The Rev. John Petty, writing a history of Primitive Methodism up to 1860, commented that the situation in Brighton: 'has never been very prosperous' although he also hoped that 'a foundation has been laid for ultimate success.' That success was to come a decade or so later during the ministry of the Rev. William Dinnick.

The picture of the Churches in Victorian Britain in general, and of Methodism in particular, as ever-increasing in membership is incorrect. Indeed between 1850 and 1855 all the Methodist connexions, except the Primitive Methodist, experienced a decline nationally in membership, and the Primitive Methodists only increased by 1,096 members over those five years.

Methodism in Brighton and Hove reflected the national pattern. The general picture is that after an initial surge there was either no growth or a decline in the mid-Victorian period. It would not be until the last quarter of the century that the churches would begin to grow again.

One feature of Methodist life in Brighton that is almost impossible to determine but it is clear from rare references that in the 1820s and 1830s both the Wesleyan and Bible Christian societies had members who were, in their own words, 'people of colour'. These were presumably descendants of slaves or ex-slaves. There were two brothers at the Bible Christian Church one of whom took the collection at the door. Only in one year in the membership list for Dorset Gardens is one person, Charlotte Hunter, described as 'coloured'. However as Charlotte Hunter occurs as a member in other years without any reference to 'colour' there may well have been others likewise not referred to. In each Society they seem to have been accepted on the same terms as everyone else.

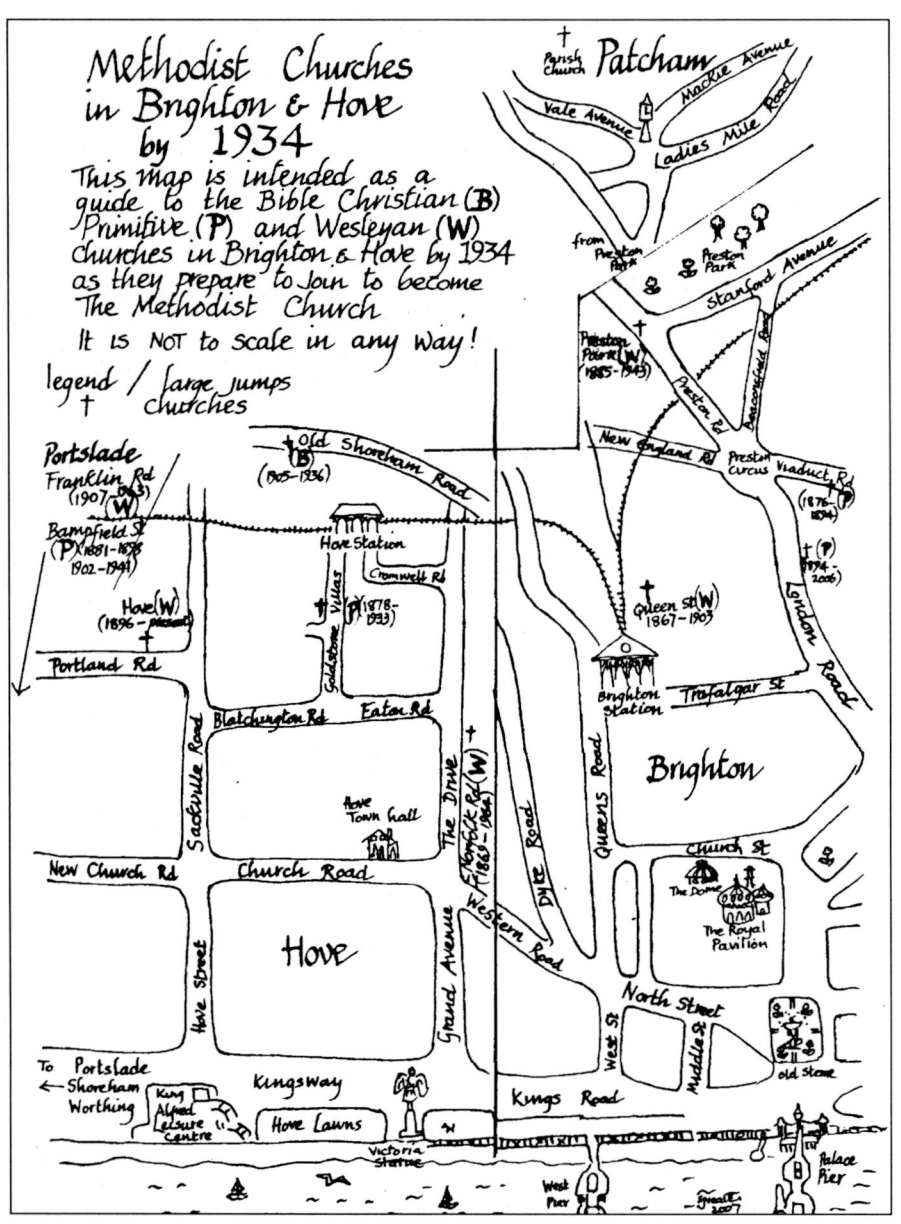

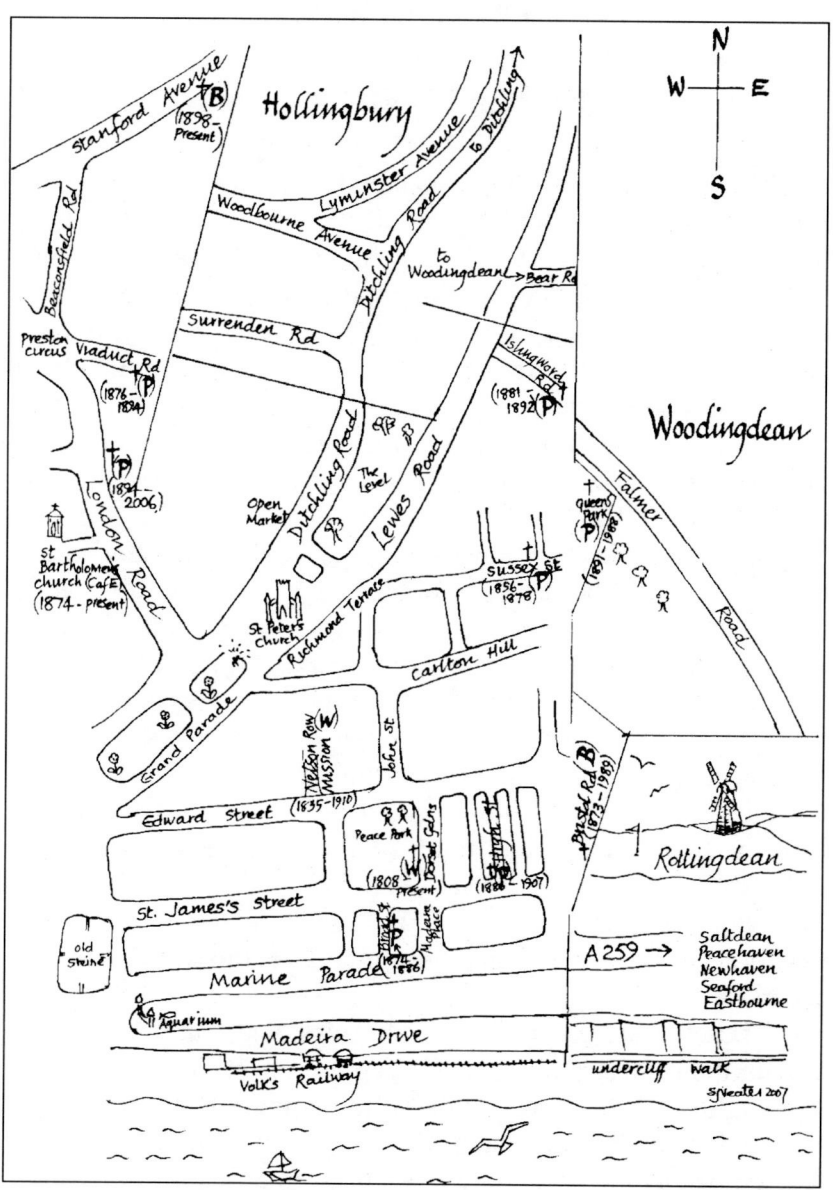

CHAPTER 4

EXPANSION and UNION – 1860-1934

The last half of the nineteenth century saw both an expansion in church building by all denominations throughout the country and a great effort in 'aggressive evangelisation'. The basis for this development lay in the concern that, according to the analysis of the 1851 census, only just over half the population attended Christian worship. In Brighton and Hove people realised that the churches had done little to reach the very poor, a situation highlighted by the publication of works such as *The Bitter Cry of Outcast London* which was published in 1883.

In response to this situation a 'Forward Movement' arose in Wesleyan Methodism. Its main leader was the Rev. Hugh Price Hughes who had been a minister at Norfolk Road in Brighton from 1872 to 1875. Two of the main features of the Forward Movement were first, the building of big Central Halls (or central missions) with large staffs which catered for all aspects of life, including entertainment. Secondly, Hughes wanted ministers to be stationed in these Missions for longer than the then current maximum period of three years. During the 1890s he urged Conference to move towards this extension, winning a vote on this matter at the 1895 Conference. By 1910 long appointments in 'missions' were the accepted practice.

These features of 'central missions' and 'extended appointments' each found their expression in the Connexions in Brighton and Hove. Indeed the situation in Wesleyan Methodism in Brighton and Hove in 1894 and 1895, which will be discussed later, may have been one of the factors that led to Hughes speaking as he did at the 1895 Conference.

Besides the 'Forward Movement' there was an added dimension to the enthusiasm for church building in Brighton and Hove. This was the impact of the Anglo-Catholic movement which has already been discussed. In reaction to the Anglo-Catholics some Anglicans were willing to finance buildings for other denominations if it meant combating what they deemed the evil of 'ritualism'. As we shall see, in the last decades of the nineteenth century the Primitive Methodists in Brighton benefited from this attitude.

The WESLEYAN METHODISTS

In many of the rapidly growing seaside resorts there was little or no Methodist presence. This was first acknowledged at the Wesleyan Conference in 1861 when it was noted that:

> '... improved mode of locomotion and changes in the habits were causing watering places to spring up all around our coasts. In some of them there was no Methodist place of worship at all; and where there was one, it bore traces of the simple time when it was built and was often entirely unattractive to persons who had grown up in surroundings of another age ...'

The Home Missionary Committee looked into the situation and reported to the 1862 Conference that there were major problems. For example, 'In Brighton, with its 100,000 inhabitants, there was but one small chapel in an obscure location'. This was the somewhat exaggerated description of Dorset Gardens. The 1862 Conference accepted an offer from the greatest Wesleyan pulpit orator of the time, the Rev. W. Morley Punshon, to travel the country over the next five years lecturing to raise £10,000 for a 'Watering-Places Chapel Fund'.

For many years the question of building in western Brighton or in Hove had been shelved, partly because of the perpetual debt on Dorset Gardens and partly because of the loss of members caused by the disruption within Wesleyan Methodism after the Conference of 1849. The rented accommodation in Windsor Street had been kept but little else had been done even though the population was still expanding westwards.

In 1861 the Rev. Jacob Stanley was appointed as superintendent minister of the Brighton circuit and, presumably in response to the concerns of Conference mentioned above, decided to act. He found that a garden of about one-tenth of an acre in Norfolk Road was for sale. Without consulting anyone and entirely on his own initiative he bought the site for £1,440 but nothing further happened for some years.

Punshon's efforts bore fruit and grants from 'Watering-Places Chapel Fund' began in 1867. Following its critique of Brighton in 1862, Wesleyan Methodism gave a very large grant of £1,000 to build what became the Norfolk Road Wesleyan Chapel. Nowhere else in the country was given a larger grant, and only that to Llandudno equalled it. With this support the foundation stone of the Norfolk Road church was laid in 1868, with almost £1,000 raised during the day's services and in the following year the society which had met at Windsor Street for over twenty years moved in.

Having expanded westwards the Wesleyans looked at the growth of Brighton northwards into the South Downs. In 1876 a 'kind friend' bought and presented to the circuit a site at the bottom of what is now Dyke Road Drive, just opposite Preston Park and a temporary iron church was erected. In 1884 a brick-built church, Preston Park Wesleyan Methodist Church, was opened.

In 1882 the Rev. Thomas Westerdale was appointed to the circuit as minister at Dorset Gardens. The *Methodist Recorder* later commented that his appointment anywhere was 'synonymous with saying that the impossible was achieved in chapel building'. Under his leadership the trustees of Dorset Gardens finally decided in 1884 to pull down the old building and construct anew on the same site.

In 1883 the iron chapel that had been used at Preston Park was moved to Bertram Road, Hove for the nascent Society there. In 1896 the current Hove Methodist Church was built on the site, now called Portland Road. Further west, the society at Portslade opened a chapel in Franklin Road, between the station and the seafront, in 1907.

The circuit was divided in 1892 because the minister at Norfolk Road, the Rev. Frank Ballard, disliked the circuit system and wanted to focus entirely on Norfolk Road. In 1894 he effectively forced the Conference to appoint him for a fourth year. The writer of the manuscript history of the Brighton Wesleyan circuit, commented upon the 1894 Conference:

> * The invitation to the Revd Frank Ballard to remain a <u>4th</u> year at Norfolk Road, was the occasion of an exciting debate, and the appointment was only secured by an evasion of the rule limiting the term of Circuit residence to 3 Years – A Note in the <u>"Minutes"</u> simply states that Frank Ballard shall reside in Brighton, and act under the direction of the Chairman of the District, so that although under that arrangement acting as Superintendent, the name of a Supernumerary Mr J. Brown stands as such – and there is nothing in the Minutes to shew that Mr Ballard has any connexion with Norfolk Road. This unique arrangement points in the direction of a future extension of the term of Residence for Circuit Ministers, and is certainly in some sense historical.
>
> * The above arrangement was <u>Continued</u> by the sanction of Conference. of 1895, held at Plymouth, after a memorable debate on the 3 Years limit of Ministerial appointment, in which Revd H. P. Hughes Drs Rigg & Perkins, and others took part – In the issue Mr Ballard was appointed for a 5th Year.

Norfolk Road thus became a one-church circuit and remained as such for almost 30 years. Ballard himself resigned from the Wesleyan ministry in January 1896 to take up a congregational pastorate in Hull. By 1907 he had returned to Wesleyan Methodism and was made 'Connexional Evidence Missioner'.

It was from Norfolk Road that the idea of hiring a theatre for evening services to attract the unchurched was developed. First, the Rev. J. Gregory Mantle hired the Alhambra Theatre but this ceased in 1901 on his departure. Secondly, the Rev. E.

Aldom French, having restarted work at the Alhambra in 1905 decided in 1907 to hire the Dome in Brighton. This vast auditorium had been the stables for the Prince Regent and was in 1907 the largest theatre/hall in Brighton or Hove, seating 1,700. Services had to stop from December 1914 because of World War I and were restarted only in 1921, in spite of the opposition of the Superintendent minister! This work became known as the 'Dome Mission'.

Also in 1921 the two circuits reunited, but the Dome Mission itself was transferred from Norfolk Road to the care of Dorset Gardens which embarked upon large extensions to make it into the equivalent of a Central Hall; these were opened in 1930.

No one from the circuit candidated for the ministry before 1860, but between 1870 and 1910 three men did so and three women became the equivalent of a deaconess in Brighton and Hove.

In 1857 Wesleyan Methodism in Brighton had one purpose-built church and one hired room with a membership of 267. It seemed to be weighed down by the debt at Dorset Gardens and the impact of the divisions following the 1849 Conference. By 1934 Wesleyanism in Brighton and Hove had five purpose-built churches together with the Dome Mission, and a total membership in the two circuits of 1,205. This number included the small societies at Hurstpierpoint and Southwick.

The BIBLE CHRISTIANS

In 1860 the Bible Christians in Brighton were struggling to survive. Unfortunately the connexional authorities seemed to regard the Brighton station as a 'circuit of ease' for 'enfeebled ministers' which hardly helped matters, especially as it was not 'easy'. By 1870 there were fewer than 40 members left in the circuit. It was with the criterion of 'ease' in mind that the Conference of 1870 decided to send to Brighton the Rev. Jehu Martin who was at Chichester at the time recovering from a severe illness and was presumably therefore deemed 'enfeebled'.

However, the dire situation in Brighton spurred Martin to vigorous activity. He bought a site for a new chapel and worked tirelessly, apparently visiting about 7,000 people in the neighbourhood, explaining what he wanted to do for the area and getting much support from 'all shades of religious persuasion'. The architect, Thomas Lainson, was so impressed by Martin's activity that he gave his services free.

Martin served for eight years, until 1878, easily the longest ministerial appointment in Brighton at that time of any Methodist connexion. After a brief spell, this pattern was repeated with the Rev. Samuel Browne Lane serving for nineteen years from 1893 to his death in 1912.

It was under Lane that the next expansions took place. First, the Bible Christians built in the growing northern suburbs in the same kind of area as the Wesleyan Preston Park Church. This church was opened in 1898 and is the current Stanford Avenue Methodist Church. Secondly, they moved west into Hove and the Old Shoreham Road Bible Christian Church was opened in 1905.

In 1907 the Bible Christians united with the Methodist New Connexion and the United Methodist Free Church to form the United Methodist Church. As there were none of the other Connexions in Brighton and Hove the Bible Christians continued as before but under a new name.

The Rev. Samuel Browne Lane
Bible Christian Superintendent minister
Brighton and Hove, 1893-1912.

In 1860 the Bible Christians had one rather poor building and a membership of about 40. Its very existence seemed in doubt and it may well have suffered the fate, referred to in the last chapter, of the United Methodist Free Church at Queen Street had it not continued to have the support of the Bible Christian Conference and the appointment of the Rev. Jehu Martin. By 1934 they had three churches and a membership of 326. It was a great recovery.

The PRIMITIVE METHODISTS

In 1861 the membership of the Primitive Methodist society in Brighton was 32 and the Quarterly Meeting reported that the spiritual state was "painfully low". A year later a local preacher was about to be reprimanded for not taking a collection at one of his services only to defend himself successfully by pointing out that there had been no congregation.

Various attempts were made to extend the work. They tried to get a room in Windsor Street near to the Wesleyans who objected very strongly placing such pressure on the landlord that he could not let them have the premises. It was only after the Wesleyans had moved to Norfolk Road that the Primitive Methodists obtained the room.

It should be noted that for many years the relationship between the Primitive Methodists and other nonconformist Churches in Brighton and Hove, including the other Methodist Connexions, was not always good. At times the Primitive Methodists seemed to act quite provocatively, for example trying to get a room in Windsor Street where the Wesleyans already had a hall and later renting a room within a stone's throw of Dorset Gardens Wesleyan Methodist Church.

The 1870s saw what Griffin calls 'much manoeuvring of meeting places' in Brighton, with at least eight different places being used, given up and occasionally re-used. The 1876 Conference compounded the matter by creating two circuits only to restore the status quo the following year.

However, 1876 also saw the arrival of the Rev. William Dinnick. One of seven brothers, five of whom were Primitive Methodist ministers, he came from a ministry in Ramsgate with a reputation for building churches. He remained in Brighton for 25 years and completely transformed the situation. In six years he built: 'eight chapels at a total cost of some £12,000, not less than £10,000 of which he raised himself.'

The Rev. William Dinnick
Primitive Methodist Superintendent minister
Brighton and Hove, 1876-1901.

Seven of these were:
1876   Viaduct Road, Brighton
        Which was near the railway works, quite possibly to counter the Anglo-Catholic mission at St. Bartholomew's:
1877   Haywards Heath
1878   Goldstone Villas, Hove
1879   Southwick
1880   Shoreham
1881   Bampfield Street, Portslade
1881   Islingword Road, Brighton

This frenetic activity should not hide the fact that Dinnick also closed places that were clearly not working, this included the first Primitive Methodist church in the county, Sussex Street in Brighton, which closed in 1878.

The support and money raised for these ventures by no means came solely from within Primitive Methodism. Over a third of the money for Viaduct Road was given by Anglicans, one of whom, T. A. Denny of London, stated that he felt:

> 'fully convinced that the Mission ... in Brighton, is the best agency that can be used to counteract the evils of Romanism, Superstition, Infidelity and other sins in the Town.'

The effort was also supported by Baptists and Congregationalists. One of the most prominent Anglican supporters was Miss E. E. Hornbuckle who, in 1881, paid the whole cost of the Islingword Road Church, a total of £750 and in 1884 paid off the whole debt of £1,000 on the Broad Street Mission Hall.

In 1894 the society at Viaduct Road moved to what became the London Road Church, built next door to the clergy house for St. Bartholomew's. The Vicar of St. Bartholomew's threatened legal action to prevent the building of the church but this was strongly resisted by Dinnick and nothing came of it.

Meanwhile in Kemp Town in 1886 the society that had met in Broad Street moved to a new church in High Street, very close to the Dorset Gardens Wesleyan Methodist Church. However, this closed in 1907. In 1891 the society at the Islingword Road Chapel moved to a new church in Queen's Park Road. It seems likely that most of the High Street society moved to Queen's Park when High Street closed in 1907.

Even after Dinnick's death in harness in January 1901 the Primitive Methodists sought to extend their work. Following the Wesleyans and the Bible Christians they thought about building a church in the growing suburbs in the north of the town and spent some years looking at the possibility of building on a the corner of Preston Drove and Beaconsfield Villas only to conclude that it was not a viable proposition. From that time onwards nothing new was attempted although in the early 1930s the circuit bought land in Patcham, once a separate parish some miles north of Brighton, but now gradually being subsumed, with the intention of building a church there.

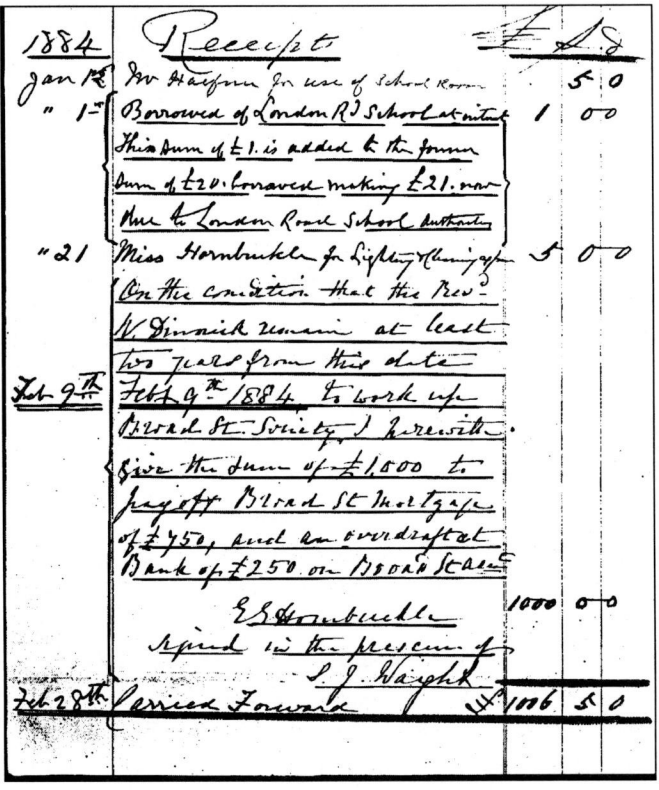

Page from Trustees Book, Broad Street Primitive Methodist Mission Hall, 1884 showing a gift of £1,000 from
Miss E. E. Hornbuckle to pay off the mortgage and overdraft

In 1860 the Primitive Methodists had one very poor building and a membership of about 30. It was in a very similar state to that of the Bible Christians. William Dinnick's arrival changed the situation dramatically and by 1934 they had three churches, London Road, Queen's Park and Bampfield Street, Portslade, the church at Goldstone Villas having closed in 1933, with a membership of 188. Most of the churches that Dinnick had built had either been merged with others that he built or had been unable to sustain themselves.

The strongest societies were those which found a base in a working community like the railway workers in the London Road area. In the period 1875-1900 those connected with the railway provided the largest group of families (20%) who had Primitive Methodist baptisms, easily outnumbering those whose fathers were described as 'labourers'.

Even so Primitive Methodism struggled even more than the other Methodist Connexions in an area such as Brighton and Hove. One of the reasons for this was that the Primitive Methodists appealed to the poorer sections of the community more than either the Wesleyans or the Bible Christians both of whom, in Brighton and Hove by the 1880s, had greater strength amongst the shop-keepers and lodging-house keepers.

The Primitive Methodist constituency was challenged from the 1880s onwards by the Salvation Army and Griffin notes that 'many members ... seceded' to this new force. However, under Dinnick's guidance, the Primitive Methodists continued their work and 'came through'.

All three Methodist Connexions in Brighton in 1860 were weak, the Bible Christians and Primitive Methodists, especially so. However, with connexional support and some very hard work, especially by ministers serving for well past the 'three-year' maximum term, by the time the three Connexions in Brighton and Hove united in 1934 they were in a far stronger position.

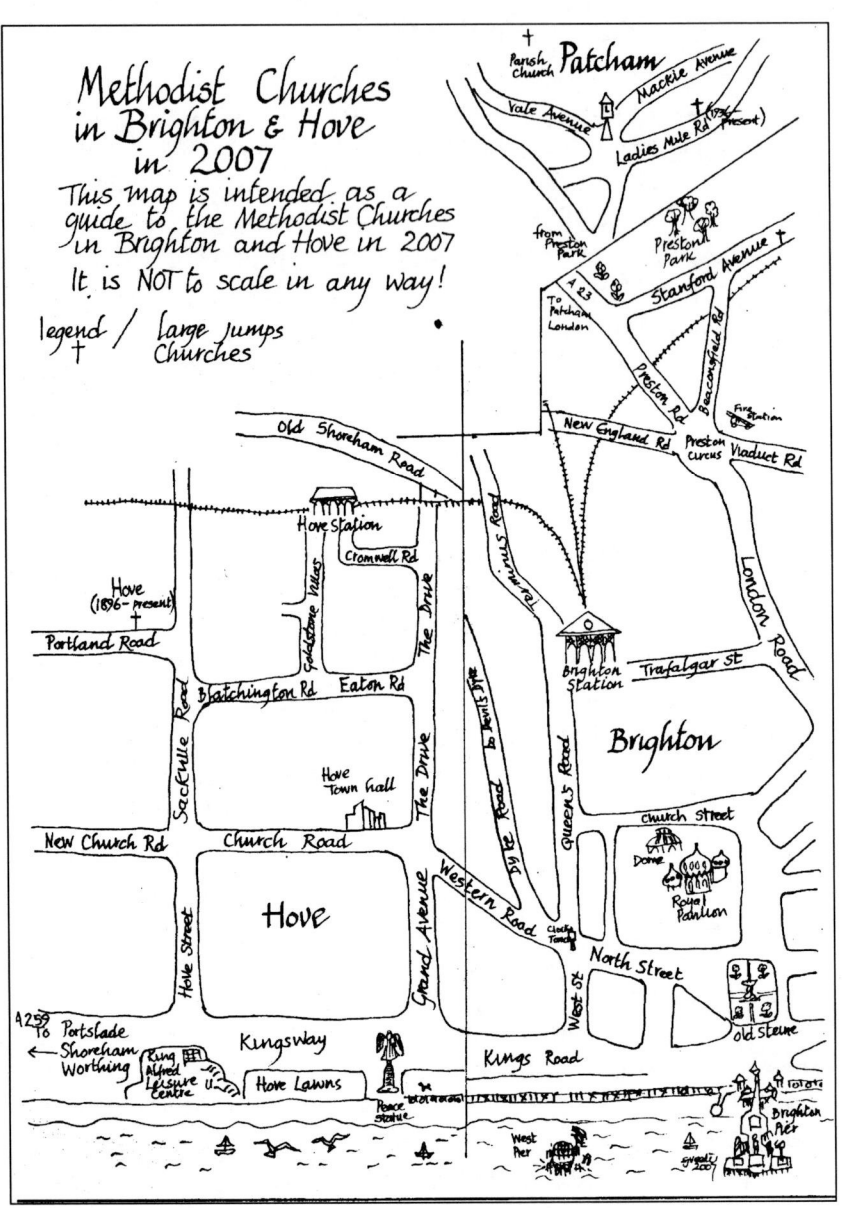

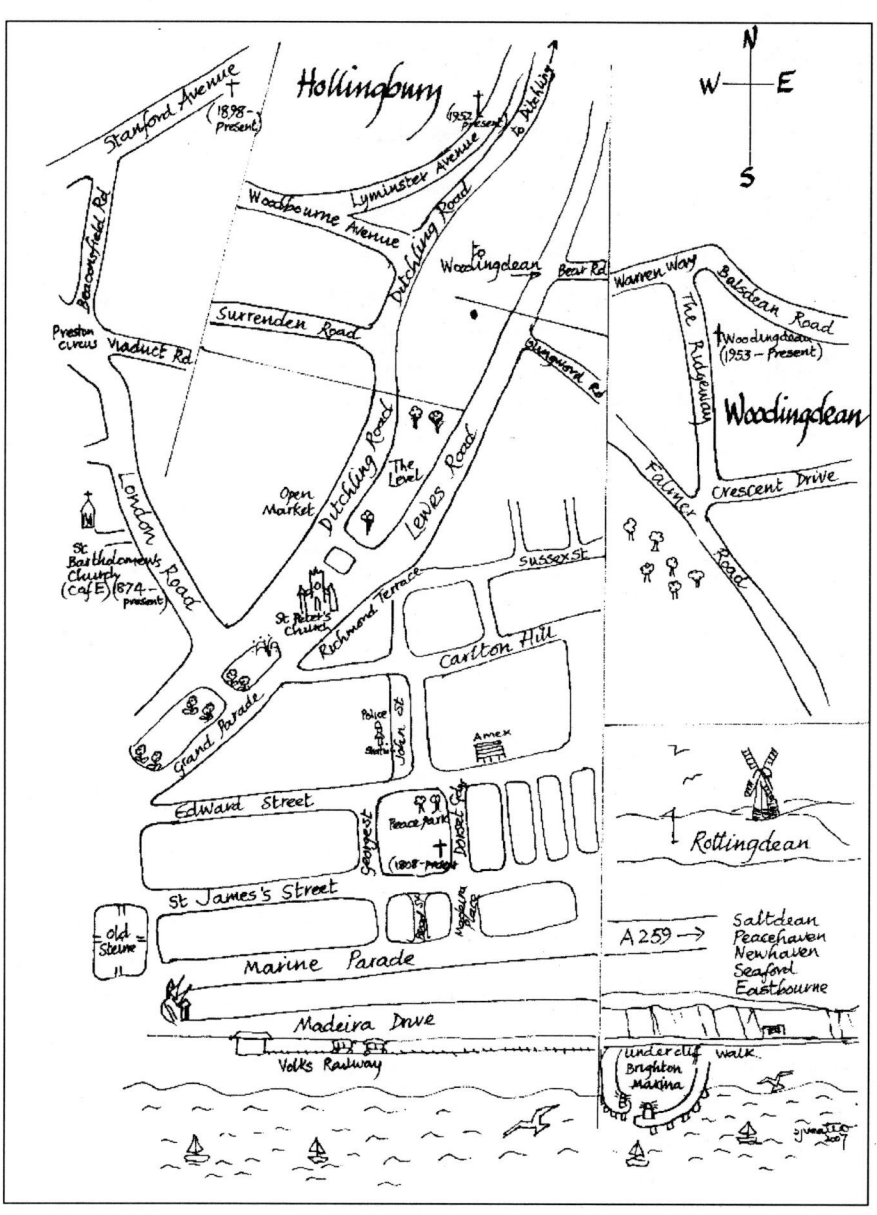

CHAPTER 5

FROM UNION ONWARDS – 1934-2007

Union between the Wesleyan Methodists, the Primitive Methodists and the United Methodists was achieved nationally in 1932. Each area was encouraged to organise itself and Brighton and Hove achieved amalgamation relatively quickly, holding its first Quarterly Meeting in September 1934. However, the phrase should be Quarterly Meetings. Although the three Connexions in Brighton and Hove seem to have had little trouble in coming together there was a disagreement within the Wesleyan community. Dorset Gardens with the Dome Mission wanted independent status, almost definitely as they did not want the Dome evening service to be part of the normal Methodist preaching Plan, preferring to keep the same preacher each week. This caused much controversy but in the end, as Griffin puts it: '… when at last the fires of debate had died down and the smoke had cleared away they stood apart …'

There were attempts over the next 60 years to bring the two circuits together, with several District Commissions, the first in 1938 and the last in the late 1980s. All such attempts foundered on the wish of the Dorset Gardens circuit to keep the Dome Mission as a distinctive area of work which they thought would not fit the pattern of the normal Methodist structure. It was only when the Dome Mission evening service was no longer viable that the two circuits finally merged in 1997.

Although they were separate circuits the relationship between the two seems to have been good and they planned their further expansion into the growing suburbs so as not to interfere with each other.

The Brighton & Hove circuit had inherited the Primitive Methodist plan and property in Patcham. They sold the property and hired the Drove Barn in Ladies Mile Road holding the first services there in 1935. A purpose-built church was opened on the site in 1969 and greatly extended and refurbished in several stages until it was completed in 2006.

Patcham Methodist Church in 2007

A Conference Commission visited the Brighton & Hove circuit in 1948 to investigate the possibilities in developing work in the post-war housing estates to the north of Brighton and Hove. In 1949 a Society was formed at Mile Oak an estate to the north of old Portslade on the western side of the circuits and a lay pastor appointed. This Society used a series of halls and in 1956 an effort was made to buy a suitable site for a church but eventually it was decided that the work in Mile Oak was not viable and the Society ceased.

A meeting held at the Patcham Church in 1950 decided to build a church in Hollingbury, a recently built housing estate in the north of Brighton, about a mile from the Patcham Church. This was opened in 1952, the finance coming partly from the sale of the ex-United Methodist Old Shoreham Church which had closed in 1936, the building having been sold in 1950.

Hollingbury Methodist Church in 2007

    The Brighton (Dome Mission) circuit looked north-eastwards to the growing estate of Woodingdean. They bought a site in 1950 and the building was opened for worship on 11 July, 1953 by Mrs E. D. Stafford of the Brighton and Hove circuit. This site was much extended and a new church was opened in May, 1986 by the Rev. the Lord Soper.

    In all three cases the first building was in the form of a 'church hall'. Both Patcham and Woodingdean eventually extended their premises to create a 'church' and a 'church hall'. Hollingbury was never able to do this.

Woodingdean Methodist Church in 2007

Whilst there was development in suburbia there was contraction of the work in the town centre, mainly due to a changing population pattern. One of these changes reflected the developing nature of shop ownership. Norfolk Road Church was on the border of Brighton and Hove on Western Road, the main shopping street that stretched from central Brighton to central Hove. The great majority of shops in the late nineteenth and early twentieth century were family businesses. A number of these families like the Andrews (Boot & Trunkmaker), Hetheringtons (Drapers), Paddisons (Fancy Drapers), Staffords (Fancy Stationers) and Vokins (Drapers) were Wesleyan Methodist. Dorothy Patching still recalls the shop workers who 'lived over the shop' during the 1920s and 1930s and who were expected to attend worship on Sundays. Naturally they tended to go to the church that the owners attended. The nature of the 'high street' changed with a decreasing number of family firms and an increasing number of nationally based companies, together with far fewer shop-workers 'living-in'. Consequently this feature of Methodist life disappeared.

Norfolk Road Church, which had been known as 'the Methodist Cathedral of the South' closed in 1964. The minister in his last address pointed out that, 'the church was built in an area of large family houses. Now it is in the midst of a no-man's-land of bed-sitter tenants and holidaymakers, who are constantly on the move,' and the headline in the *Evening Argus* was 'Congregation moves away'. The *Brighton and Hove Herald* pointed out that the organ would go to Southwick where a new church was being built.

Population movement had already had an effect on the church at Franklin Road Church, Portslade with the loss of over half its members in twenty years. It was decided that they too had to close and its last service was held in May, 1963. Most of the congregation joined either Hove or Southwick.

In the late 1960s there was a suggestion that Bristol Road should close. Only six of its 34 members lived in the area, but after a determined effort they continued for another twenty years.

The shortage of ministers in Methodism caused the staff in the Brighton & Hove circuit to be reduced by one. As a consequence in the east of Brighton, Bristol Road Church and Queen's Park Church were transferred from the Brighton & Hove circuit to the Brighton (Dome Mission) circuit and welcomed into their new circuit at a service at the Dome on 19 July, 1981. However both churches were within a quarter of a mile of Dorset Gardens and their societies were small (in 1984 Bristol Road had 35 members, and Queen's Park had 25 members). In addition the building at Queen's Park was deteriorating, apparently having been constructed with 'sea-sand which attracted dampness'. For many years the services there had taken place in the hall underneath the church itself.

A District Re-development Committee met the Brighton (Dome Mission) circuit in 1984 and recommended a serious consideration of the three old buildings in Kemp Town (Bristol Road, Dorset Gardens and Queen's Park), and the circuit undertook a review. The Queen's Park society decided that they had to leave the building and, whilst retaining membership of the Dome Mission circuit, they moved to worship at London Road Church, in the Brighton & Hove circuit, taking the evening service there. When the two circuits united in 1997 the remaining members joined other churches in the new circuit and the Queen's Park society came to an end.

There was some disquiet within the Bristol Road Society, in 1986 the Church Council asked to move back to the Brighton & Hove circuit. Eventually, following a further District Re-development Committee in 1988, a decision was taken that they too could no longer maintain themselves and the final service took place on 9 July, 1989.

The Dome Mission itself was encountering problems with the change in the pattern of worship and of Sunday evening activities in general. As Len Wright in his history of the Dome Mission in 1985 commented, '(t)he televised *Forsyte Saga* series has a lot to answer for.' He also commented on the 'astronomic' increases in bus fares and the fact that people were increasingly living out of the town centre. In addition to declining congregations the town authorities wanted to use the Dome on Sunday evenings more for their own activities and the costs were increasing, for example the extra cost of security in the wake of the bombing of the Grand Hotel in 1984. The use of the Dome for regular weekly services ended in 1985 in favour of monthly worship together with special events such as the Christmas Carol Service.

Dorset Gardens, with a large membership but with a concern about its building, at first looked at building a completely new church, a 'theatre church' which would combine the work both of Dorset Gardens and the Dome Mission. A nearby site was acquired at the bottom of Edward Street on the main thoroughfare into Brighton. However, after many trials and tribulations it was decided not to proceed with this project but instead to demolish the Dorset Gardens Church and build a smaller church on the site, with housing occupying the remainder. By this time it was clear that the Dome evening service was increasingly difficult to sustain and the last Dome service, the Christmas Carol Service, took place in 1998.

Dorset Gardens Church was demolished and work began in 2001 on building anew. The Dorset Gardens congregation shared work and worship at London Road Methodist Church whilst the building took place. This took almost two years to complete. The congregation moved back in December 2002 with the new church being opened on Saturday, 5 April, 2003 by the Rev. Dr. Colin Morris.

Dorset Gardens Methodist Church in 2007

The London Road Church had had a falling membership for some years and in 1989 there were moves in the Brighton and Hove circuit to close the Church but these did not come to fruition at that time. However, the decline of the local population base continued and in 2005 the Society decided that it could no longer continue and a decision was made to close the Church, the last of a Primitive Methodist foundation in Brighton and Hove, in May 2006.

By this time the two circuits had merged and in September 1997 there was only one Methodist circuit in Brighton and Hove. At the merger, Southwick moved to the Worthing circuit thereby making the boundary of the circuit coterminous with the new unitary authority of Brighton and Hove. The society at Hurstpierpoint had left the Brighton & Hove circuit in 1963 to join the Sussex Mission, soon to become the Mid-Sussex circuit, having been part of the Brighton & Hove circuit for 130 years.

The story of Methodism in the post-war period is one of initial expansion into the suburbs and then a retreat from the centre of the city where the resident population was in increasing decline. The only exception was Dorset Gardens which was unusual in that, following its Dome Mission tradition, it felt itself more in the 'Central Hall' mould. As such it was a 'gathered church' with its members and congregation coming from across the city and beyond to serve what it saw as the needs of the local area. The other churches functioned far more as the local Methodist church of their area.

This move away from the city centre to the suburbs mirrors the move of the secondary schools. A recent map in the local paper, the *Argus*, shows a similar distribution of schools to Methodist churches. Obviously there is no direct correlation but each has the same cause, the movement of population.

CHAPTER 6

BUILDINGS and FINANCE 1807-2007

BUILDINGS

In the design of places of worship John Wesley, as in so many other areas of Methodist life, knew what he wanted and wrote it down. His preference was for octagonal chapels as they were 'best for the voice'. Failing that he preferred a 'square house after the model of Bath or Scarborough'. In his study of Methodist architecture George Dolby points out that there is no tradition within Christianity of building square chapels and thinks that it must have been a specifically Methodist development. Dolby goes on to mention that 'in the nineteenth century there are quite a number of square-planned Methodist chapels' and gives the examples of Belper (1807) and Thirsk (1816). He could easily have included Dorset Gardens Wesleyan Methodist chapel, built in 1808, for it too 'was square, constructed in red brick, with round topped windows'.

As an aside it should be noted that the Woodingdean Church which was opened in 1986 is 'square' thus returning, probably unwittingly, to Wesley's principles.

Insofar as its financial resources allowed Methodism was influenced by the prevailing architectural taste in British society. In the early nineteenth century there was a revival of interest in Greek forms whereas by the middle of the century Gothic was deemed to be the 'correct' form. The Wesleyan minister, F. J. Jobson, who had trained as an architect, wrote in 1850 that Gothic architecture is 'English Church architecture'. It was also, he pointed out, the 'most economic style of Chapel Building'.

Undoubtedly these factors underlay the changes in the appearance of Dorset Gardens in 1823 when the building was much enlarged and given a frontage which 'was handsomely finished with a Pediment and Pilaster with Corinthian Capitals'.

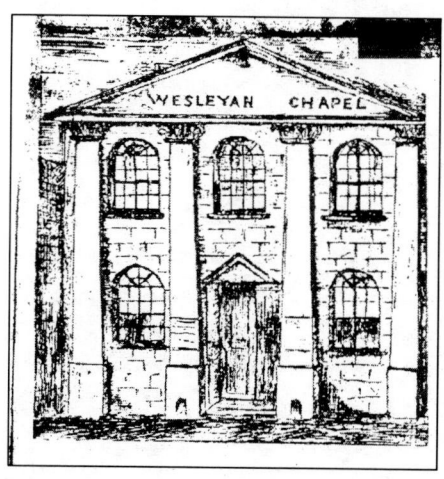

Sketch of Dorset Gardens 'Wesleyan Chapel' showing the 'Corinthian Capitals' made between 1827 and 1884 by Richard W. Jennings. Published in the *Brighton Herald* 12 September, 1931

This classical Greek design was replaced in 1884 by an Italianate design, called 'Free Renaissance' by Elleray in his description of *The Victorian Churches of Sussex*. This design was common for major buildings in Brighton at the time, such as the Grand Hotel and the Brighton Aquarium which was opened in 1872. Dorset Gardens Church was designed by a well-known architect from Liverpool, C. O. Ellison. Ellison also designed the Wesleyan church at Norfolk Road in 1868 but this was built in an Early English Gothic style with stone and flint dressing. Ellison must have been favoured by the Wesleyan community because he also designed the Church at Preston Park in 1883. Like Dorset Gardens it had red-brick terracotta, but unlike Dorset Gardens was built in the Gothic style.

Dorset Gardens Wesleyan Methodist Church 1885

Preston Park Wesleyan Methodist Church from C. O. Ellison's sketch, c. 1883

1896 Hove managed to combine the two styles: being described by Elleray as 'Gothic Romanesque', although the *Brighton Herald* called its style 'Transitional, between the Norman and Early English Gothic'. It was the first Wesleyan church in Brighton and Hove in over 30 years not to have been designed by Ellison.

Hove Methodist Church in 2007.
On the right the front of the Church has been altered to make access easier. Further building has been added at the rear, on the left. Otherwise the central structure is at it was designed in the 1890s.

As has been stated, this move from 'square' to 'Greek' and from 'Greek' to 'Gothic' style in architecture in Brighton and Hove is a reflection of a move throughout all the Methodist connexions nationally, indeed throughout Nonconformity in the latter nineteenth century. This move was described by James Munson in *The Nonconformists* as, 'the search for dignity' and he comments that '(T)he victory of Gothic architecture showed that Nonconformity had kept pace with the spirit of the times.'

The Bible Christians also followed this development. Bristol Road was designed in a Romanesque style in 1872, but both Stanford Avenue (opened in 1898) and Old Shoreham Road (opened in 1905) were designed by E. J. Hamilton in an Early English Gothic style.

Bristol Road Bible Christian Church, opened in 1873. This must be an artist's impression.

In contrast both London Road and Queen's Park Primitive Methodist churches were in the Free Renaissance style. This may well be due to the relative lack of wealth within Primitive Methodism which by 1901 had a debt nationally of over £1 million.

However all of these Churches, except Queen's Park, were either built with or, in the case of London Road, soon acquired, a tower. Norfolk Road Wesleyan Methodist Church had a tall spire on top of its tower. A tower added nothing functionally to any of the buildings, as bells were not used to summon people to worship, rather they were an expression of the wish to be 'respectable'. Even the Bible Christians, who at first had a strongly puritanical approach to all things of 'show', followed this trend. In 1851 the Brighton Quarterly Meeting stated that it wanted a 'good chapel in a respectable part of town'.

London Road Primitive Methodist Church before 1910.

The interior design of each building was relatively plain, especially in the early phase of each church. The basic design was to have pews facing a large pulpit which was above a communion table. In the larger churches such as Dorset Gardens and Hove there was a gallery. Both Preston Park Wesleyan Methodist Church and Stanford Avenue Bible Christian Church had transepts. The dominant feature of these nineteenth century buildings was the pulpit which was placed centrally at the far wall with the preacher looking down on the congregation.

There was one notable exception to this pattern. Norfolk Road Wesleyan Methodist Church had a central aisle with the communion table as the focal point. The lectern and the pulpit were both to the side and ornate. To any casual observer distinguishing Norfolk Road from the Church of England would have been difficult, especially as the liturgy would also have been almost identical

Stanford Avenue Methodist Church, c. 2004 showing the apse and transepts.

Interior of Hove Methodist Church showing the central, raised pulpit, 2007.

Norfolk Road Wesleyan Methodist Church
showing the central communion table and side pulpit.

A wedding at Norfolk Road Methodist Church in the 1950s showing the
choir stalls and the steps up to them.

Decoration in the early buildings was almost non-existent, the accounts of Dorset Gardens refer commonly to whitewash. Paint, or 'colouring' as it was called, is first mentioned in 1849. However, gradually things changed and stained glass began to appear for example in Hove Wesleyan Methodist Church in 1896. The Bible Christians also developed a more ornate style of decoration and Bristol Road was designed in 1872 with, 'coloured brick with ornamental dressings at the windows and doorways and an ornate interior'.

The Primitive Methodists retained the plainer approach throughout the nineteenth century. Partly this was a matter of cost, they built more churches in Brighton and Hove in the last quarter of the century than the Wesleyans and Bible Christians combined, yet with a smaller membership.

London Road Primitive Methodist Church in c. 1910. The plaque above the door on the right is in memory of the Rev. W. Dinnick who died in 1901. Otherwise the interior is devoid of decoration.
The white cards in the pews were for the names of those who had rented that pew.

There was also a strong tradition of simplicity, shared by the Bible Christians in their rural communities. In Brighton and Hove there was also the sense of being completely different from the Anglo-Catholic churches like St. Bartholomew's, with which they were in competition. At the opening of London Road in 1895 Alderman Martin remarked that 'the bright and happy faces of Christian souls was all the decoration truly needed.'

Even so, decoration arose in the Primitive churches. This usually came about as a memorial to those who had served the church and, after 1918, those had died in the war, or as a thanksgiving for those who had returned. These ideas were behind the windows of 'leaded cathedral glass' at London Road unveiled in 1921. Bristol Road too had a war memorial of fine stained glass windows placed in the Church in 1920.

By the beginning of the twenty-first century concepts of decoration in Methodist churches had undergone a complete change from two centuries earlier. One of the distinctive features of the new Dorset Gardens church opened in 2003 is the stained glass window designed by local artist and church member, Shirley Veater.

One of the main reasons for these changes was the Liturgical Movement which began to have a major impact after World War II. This movement, which affected all western Churches including the Roman Catholic Church, sought amongst other things, to encourage greater participation by the whole congregation in the act of worship and reminded Christians of their common liturgical heritage especially Holy Communion.

Hollingbury Methodist Church during its 40th anniversary celebrations, 1992. The pulpit is moveable.

One of the immediate effects in Brighton and Hove can be seen in the design of the three churches built after Methodist Union: Hollingbury (1952), Patcham (1936, new building 1969 and 2006), and Woodingdean (1953, new building 1986). These were all based on a church hall design with chairs rather than pews. In each the pulpit was moved to the side and the focal point became the communion table. This design was also adopted by Stanford Avenue in its new interior opened in 1991, and for the new Dorset Gardens which was opened in 2003. London Road was closed in 2005 and so Hove alone retains the nineteenth century design. Neither Dorset Gardens nor Woodingdean now use communion rails. Other churches such as Hove have moveable rails.

Patcham Methodist Church, 2007. The communion table is placed centrally.

Many Methodist churches have a large number of rooms other than the area set aside for worship. These included rooms such as a vestry, added to Dorset Gardens in 1811, and places for meetings, especially for groups such as a Sunday School. One of the reasons for the number of rooms is that the local Methodist church increasingly became the focus of a way of life called 'the chapel culture'. This led to large numbers of activities other than worship taking place on the premises, and such activities needed rooms. We shall look at this aspect in a later chapter.

One of the problems in Brighton and Hove is the lack of building space and many nineteenth century buildings had rooms in the basement. These were often used for the Sunday school which led to self-criticism by the local Wesleyans in 1904 when they stated, rather sternly, that it hoped that 'the days are past when Sunday Schools will be allowed to meet in "dens and caves of the earth," where adequate head-room, lighting, and ventilation are impossible.' As Smith and Nurcombe point out in their history of Hove Methodist Church, '[T]he shortage of land necessitated this style of building'.

All churches in the centre of Brighton and Hove faced this problem. Some, like London Road, had a hall behind the church, but most had had to have multi-level buildings. The new Dorset Gardens Church is built on three floors with the church at the top, but avoids having any Sunday school in a 'basement'.

The post-union Churches were all erected in the developing suburbs on the Downs. Both Patcham and Woodingdean were able to build most or all rooms on the same single level so that stairs and access are not a great problem. Hollingbury was built into the side of a hill so that the room(s) under the Church is not a 'basement', but is entered from open land. Dorset Gardens, Hove and Stanford Avenue have each had to adapt their premises by the use of lifts or ramps to ensure access for all.

Stanford Avenue Methodist Church in 2007, showing the access ramp

FINANCE

Until 1976 all Methodist buildings were run by Trustees. The Trustees had to raise the money to build the church, although this was often done in Brighton and Hove by the minister, e.g. Thomas Westerdale for the Wesleyans at Dorset Gardens, Jehu Martin for the Bible Christians at Bristol Road and William Dinnick for the Primitive Methodists everywhere. The other responsibility of the Trustees was the running of the building and taking care of its upkeep.

One very important factor for Methodism in Brighton and Hove is that there has never been a very large employer in the town and consequently no very rich nineteenth century businessman to fund any of the branches of Methodism in the area. Brighton and Hove had no Wesleyan like Jesse Boot of Nottingham (founder of Boots) and no Primitive Methodist like Sir William Hartley (founder of Hartley's Jam). It is significant that in the 1881 census only one of the resident Trustees of any of the Methodist connexions in Brighton and Hove who can be identified had more than one living-in servant. He was Edward Beves, grandson of Edward Beves the effective father of Wesleyan Methodism in Brighton, who had four such servants. The largest employer in the group in 1881 was a Wesleyan Methodist 'fancy draper', William Paddison, who had nine employees living on the premises at the time.

All Methodist connexions in Brighton and Hove have always had to fund their activities without recourse to the wealthy Methodist who could pay from a personal cheque-book. The only exception to this was when the Primitive Methodists under William Dinnick had recourse to the personal wealth of a local Anglican, Miss E. E. Hornbuckle, who, as we saw earlier, in 1881 paid the whole cost of the Islingword Road Church and paid off the debt on the Broad Street Mission Hall, as well as giving large donations for other churches.

In the nineteenth century the running of the large majority of churches of all denominations in Brighton and Hove was financed by renting pews to members of the congregation. Of the 38 places of Christian worship in Brighton at the 1851 religious census only ten had no pew rents and most of these were small independent chapels. With the exception of the Quakers all those who had seating for 400 or more had pew rents for some or most of the seating. Most churches rented out over half the seating capacity and all the churches of the Church of England had pew rents. One of the features of Brighton church life was the number of proprietary chapels, both of the Church of England and of other denominations. These were built to attract a congregation and therefore an income. The highest income in 1851 was for St. Margaret's Church in the Church of England which had a gross annual rental of over £800.00 p.a. It so happens that the eventual owner of this church would be Miss Hornbuckle who was so instrumental in the spread of Primitive Methodism in the 1880s.

It was the Anglo-Catholic movement in the Church of England which built churches without renting pews and thereby led the way for the eventual abolition of all pew rents. It was the existence of pew rents that led to adverts for the Dome Mission stating, 'All seats free', long after pew rents themselves had disappeared, for the memory lingered. Most if not all nineteenth century Methodist churches had pew rents but they disappeared by the middle of the twentieth century. The last record of a Methodist church in Brighton and Hove abolishing its pew rents was London Road in 1955. The weekly 'free-will' offering by everyone replaced the pew rent.

Whilst the 'pew rent' might seem odd to modern thinking it meant that poor people paid nothing at all, because all churches had a number of 'free seats'. When 'collections' replaced the 'pew rent' there were some objections that it was a burden on the poor. Pew rent was however, inequitable. The best seats were those which were rented out and those who like to 'sit at the back' in worship today might like to consider that the most expensive pews were those near the front of the church. In addition, 'seat-holders' were given a say in the decision-making of the church even though they might not be members there. For example the Trustees at Dorset Gardens resolved in 1891 to ascertain 'the wishes of the Seatholders and Members of Society' when considering a change in worship.

The other method by which money was raised in the first half of the nineteenth century was to ask for loans and to pay off the interest each year. This was self-defeating and Dorset Gardens carried a debt for most of the nineteenth century which meant that it did not want to spend money on enabling the circuit to build elsewhere in Brighton nor, until the Rev. Thomas Westerdale arrived in 1882, on renewing itself.

Other methods were sought. First, there were the fund-raising events. The earliest of these in Brighton that can be identified was the 'Anniversary collection', in 1844. Secondly there was the idea of a public meeting with a major speaker. The earliest recorded one of these took place in 1860 when the Dorset Gardens trustees invited the leading ministerial speaker of the day, the Rev. Morley Punshon, to speak at a public meeting. This raised almost £18 which was about 10% of their total annual expenditure at the time.

To this was added 'the special tea meeting' such as that in the Pavilion Picture Gallery in 1872 to raise money for the Bristol Road Church. 'Tea' became such a feature of Methodist life that it soon became almost synonymous with Methodism. Equally famous were events such as the bazaar, that at Stanford Avenue Bible Christian church in 1898 raised over 10% of the total cost of the building. Dorothy Baker of Dorset Gardens recalls that the bazaar was, 'a great day of the year'.

After World War II other fund raising ventures such as sponsored events were used. In the 1980s David Rutter ran marathons for the Dome Mission and the minister at Patcham, the Rev. Doug Hopwood, had his beard shaved off to raise money in the 1990s.

For much of the twentieth century and into the present century the major money-raising activity was the 'Anniversary'. This annual event became a highlight of Church life with a printed report of the previous year, and a programme of events including a 'rally' with 'major' preachers. One of the features of the occasion was the giving of money by both groups and individuals. Some of this giving was sacrificial. The Rev. Frank Thewlis, when he arrived at the Dome Mission in 1968, recalled that people who could ill afford it kept all their copper change through the year to give 'to God at the Anniversary'.

Money was not only raised to fund the building. Methodism has always raised money for other activities and projects and this will be dealt with elsewhere.

Methodism in Brighton and Hove in 2007 is financially far healthier than it was at any time in the nineteenth century and probably for most of the twentieth century. When the new Dorset Gardens was opened in 2003 it was the first occasion since it was first built in 1808 that a new building on the site was opened free of debt.

The different Methodist connexions in Brighton and Hove built and decorated their churches according to, or at times beyond, their means. They used the latest architectural style and followed liturgical developments. To finance their efforts Methodists used many different methods, again employing what was to hand. The idea of running a building on debt for apparently endless years, as with the early Dorset Gardens, would, we trust, no longer be contemplated.

CHAPTER 7

The SPIRITUAL LIFE of the CHURCH – I

BACKGROUND

Worship in most churches in the eighteenth century consisted of the parson reciting the prayers with responses from the clerk, reading a written sermon, and possibly the chanting of psalms. There was little hymn singing in public worship until Isaac Watts (1674-1748), a dissenter, began to write them. Most churches offered Holy Communion quarterly but, according to Currie, Gilbert and Horsley in their study of churches at this time, the great majority of the population, over 95%, did not take communion at all.

In contrast both John and Charles Wesley received communion frequently. They thought of it as a 'converting' as well as a 'confirming ordinance'. They also placed great value on 'preaching' and often did this extempore. The 1768 Conference reiterated the value of the preaching service at five in the morning and called it the 'glory of Methodism'. It was by preaching that people were brought to God.

The third main aspect of Methodist worship was its congregational singing. The early Methodist societies sang so much that the Preface to the 1933 *Methodist Hymn Book* compiled for the newly united Methodist church started with the sentence: "Methodism was born in song". Methodists were extraordinarily fortunate in that Charles Wesley was a hymn-writer of genius. Methodists sing their theology.

Methodist spiritual life was nourished by meeting weekly 'in class' where the state of each soul was examined and mutual encouragement given. All of these features were found in the development of Methodism in Brighton and Hove.

Both preaching and hymn-singing have survived John Wesley's death in 1791 to the present day, but in other areas

Methodism did not adhere fully to his legacy. For example, the class meeting gradually declined and by the latter part of the nineteenth century had ceased to be what it was under Wesley, although membership of each Connexion was still counted by being a member of a class. The Wesleyan Plans in Brighton and Hove for 1902 give the dates and times of quarterly pastoral visitations for each class, indicating that there was life in the class meeting yet, but the minute book of the Leaders' Meetings for this period shows increasing concern that all was not well. The Bible Christian class meetings in c. 1882 were, as Sawyer noted in his reports on Brighton churches in c. 1882, 'conspicuous by their absence'. By the latter part of the twentieth century 'meeting in class' had disappeared in practice in Brighton and Hove.

Preaching took precedence over sacramental worship and, as we have seen, churches in Brighton and Hove until the period after World War II were designed with the large pulpit as the focal point. Holy Communion, always termed 'the sacrament' in nineteenth plans, became a monthly, or even a quarterly or yearly event in some Methodist churches.

HOLY COMMUNION

There are very few extant Plans for the period before 1918. However, an analysis of these few together with the Town Directories from 1822-1918 shows that in Brighton and Hove in the latter part of the nineteenth century all three connexions followed the national pattern and celebrated Holy Communion in its larger churches once a month in the evening, usually at 8.00 p.m. after the evening service. In the smaller churches and the 'mission halls', like the Wesleyan Nelson Row, it is not mentioned at all.

In the earlier part of that century however the pattern was different. The two earliest Plans, both Wesleyan, for April to August, 1823 and May to October 1831 show that eucharistic practice was very rare. In 1823 there were two ministers and eighteen preaching places. Only Brighton, that is Dorset Gardens, had Holy Communion at all during these months, but six places, not Brighton, had a 'Love-feast' led by a Local Preacher. The Love-feast was introduced by John Wesley who had experienced its use by the Moravians. It is a communal meal of 'a little plain cake and water'. With the exception of the Mission at Nelson Row each Wesleyan church had a Love-feast planned in 1902.

An analysis of Preaching Plans over the last two or three decades shows that most churches in the circuit now have Holy Communion at some point on the majority of Sundays, but the Love-feast has disappeared save on very rare occasions. Some churches, Dorset Gardens, Hove and Woodingdean, have an early morning communion two or three times a quarter. In addition both Hove and Stanford Avenue have regular midweek communions.

Another change in practice is that Holy Communion will be integral to the whole act of worship and not an extra service after most worshippers have left. This development seems to have taken place in Brighton and Hove with the introduction of the Methodist Service Book in 1975. The senior Local Preacher in the circuit, Frances Timpson, noted that when she arrived in Brighton and Hove from Bristol in 1989 all churches in the Brighton & Hove circuit had Holy Communion as an integral part of worship.

A further development is the move from only giving communion to members of the Societies in the eighteenth and nineteenth centuries to the 'open table' of 'accepting all who love the Lord Jesus' during the twentieth century. It is not possible to state when this move occurred, especially as it has never been officially sanctioned by Conference as the Report on *'Children and Holy Communion (2000)'* pointed out. It is probable that the 'open table' has been the practice in at least part of Brighton and Hove since the 1950s. The superintendent minister of the Brighton (Dome Mission) circuit 1953-1967, the Rev Dr. Leslie Newman, held this idea very strongly indeed, it was one of the reasons for his rejection of the first series of talks aimed at uniting the Methodist Church and the Church of England.

Although Wesleyan Methodists in general took communion from a communion rail the Primitive Methodists followed the tradition of receiving it in the pews. It was only gradually that the ex-Primitive Methodists churches in the area followed the ex-Wesleyan practice, London Road making the change in 1958.

Since their introduction *The Methodist Service Book* (1975) and its successor *Methodist Worship* (1999) have been commonly used for Holy Communion but in the last two decades other liturgies, for example those developed by the Iona community, have also been frequently used. It is now usual for children to receive the elements. This was already the case at Woodingdean by 1980 when Richard and Beulah Fletcher arrived with their family, but was not introduced at Hove until the arrival of the Rev. Rob Hufton in 1996.

FREQUENCY and TIMING of the SERVICES

In the first part of the nineteenth century three services were held each Sunday: morning, afternoon and evening. Some, like the Bible Christian minister in the 1820s, the Rev. Billy Bailey, might preach six times each Sunday, three times outdoors and three times in the churches. In 1851 the evening service for all, except at Dorset Gardens, was the best attended. Afternoon services for the Bible Christians and the Wesleyans had disappeared by the 1860s and probably before then. The Primitive Methodists, with the exception of a couple of years early in Dinnick's ministry, never had them. However, by 1910, Wesleyan churches like Hove and Preston Park were having 'Men's Brotherhood' in the afternoon. Other churches, such as Dorset Gardens, had a 'Pleasant Sunday Afternoon', (P.S.A.) which developed their own 'slate club' and 'band'.

Weekday services including 'prayer meetings' were held throughout this period, usually two or three times a week. These might last for a long time. The first Bible Christian minister, the Rev. Andrew Cory, wrote in his diary for Tuesday, 8 March, 1825 that prayer 'meetings continued until ten, eleven, and twelve at night' having started at seven.

William Dinnick instigated a flurry of activity in Primitive Methodism from 1877 onwards by having services or prayer meetings four or five nights a week, only Saturday being left unused. This pattern returned to the 'norm' after his death in 1901. In all the different connexions the timing of the services moved to later in the day throughout the century. From 10.30 a.m. up to the 1840s to 11.00 a.m. by the 1860s. In general evening services, which were introduced to English custom by Methodists in the eighteenth century, followed this pattern, moving from 6.30 p.m. to 7.00 p.m. It was not until the 1980s that there was return to the earlier pattern in the timing of worship.

In general the evening services were intended for the uncommitted whereas the morning service was thought of as being more for the membership. During the twentieth century there was a gradual decline in the provision of and attendance at evening worship, as a greater proportion began to attend in the morning, although this was not the case at Patcham in the 1950s, and Alan Richards, a local preacher, recalls it being only marginally so at Hove in both the 1950s and 1960s. In 2007 an evening service is held every Sunday in only three of the six churches, Dorset Gardens, Patcham and Stanford Avenue: twice a month at Hove and once a month at Woodingdean. The smallest of the churches, Hollingbury, does not have an evening service.

The Dome Evening Service waiting to start. It is probably from the early-mid 1940s. Although it cannot be seen clearly the gallery is also full.

In Brighton this change is most dramatically seen in the evening services at the Dome, which regularly had congregations of between 1,500 and 2,000, especially during World War II. By the 1950s, under the Rev. Dr. Leslie Newman, the Dome had one of the largest evening congregations in the country that met Sunday by Sunday with up to 2,500 at times. However, despite the best efforts of both ministers and people, the great changes in society that we have already looked at meant a decline in attendance at these services. The Dome service has now ceased.

PREACHING

Much preaching in the early years in all the Connexions took place in the open, especially before permanent buildings were used. In the eighteenth and early nineteenth centuries the sermon may well have been in the middle of the service but by the latter part of the nineteenth century and for most of the twentieth century it was the spiritual climax of worship followed only by a hymn and a blessing. This pattern continued until the last quarter of the twentieth century when the new *Methodist Service Book (1975)* placed it far more in the centre of the service, to be followed by the 'response'. This pattern is followed in the current *Methodist Worship Book*, published in 1999. It is not possible to be exact as to when this change occurred in Brighton and Hove, partly because different preachers have different ideas, approaches and emphases. In 1989 Frances Timpson noticed that the sermon as climax was universal in the Brighton and Hove circuit, but that gradually it has changed with most now placing it more centrally. Another long-serving local preacher, Bob Hinton, has noticed from his own records how his practice changed. He often placed the sermon as the climax of worship into the late 1980s but from the 1990s onwards never did so. Some preachers retain the sermon as the climax of worship.

The style of sermon has also changed, although this too is very difficult to quantify. The early preachers in Brighton of all connexions were often preaching to people who were not Methodists. Therefore they preached for conversion and commitment. However, when preaching to the membership, aspects of Methodist doctrine would be emphasised. The Rev. John Smith who was a Wesleyan Minister in Brighton 1818-1819, preached 'frequently and empathically … on the necessity of Christian perfection'. The frequency leading to the expressed annoyance of at least one member.

Preaching for conversion remained the practice. In 1871 one Primitive Methodist minister declined to stay for a second year "as no more souls were being saved." However, Methodist doctrine was also taught although Sawyer noticed in c. 1882 that at Dorset Gardens 'perfection' was not mentioned, rather a 'full and free Gospel is preached', the sermons being 'free from sectarianism'.

Primitive Methodists also referred to doctrine. In 1881 the opening of the Islingword Road Primitive Methodist Church was attended by the Secretary of the General Missionary Committee, the Rev. Robinson Cheeseman. In what must have been a lengthy address he gave what the reporter for the Brighton Guardian called:

> 'a capital address on the Doctrines of the Church which included the Primeval Innocence of Man, his Fall, Justification by Faith, Sanctification by the Holy Spirit, the Atonement of Christ, the Doctrine of the Trinity, the Immortality of the Soul, the General Judgement and the Eternal Reward and Punishments.'

The length of the sermon has also changed over time. Sawyer in c. 1882 reported that the average time at Dorset Gardens 'is considered to be about half-an-hour'. It would be wrong however to equate the past with length. The Rev. Dr. Leslie Newman, whose quality of preaching was such that Kenneth Young in his study of nonconformist culture, *Chapel*, places him in a brief list that includes Spurgeon and Hugh Price Hughes, regularly preached at the Dome evening services from 1953 to 1967 for up to 45 minutes. His predecessor at the Dome was the Rev. Fred Pratt Green, arguably Methodism's most gifted hymn-writer since Charles Wesley. Green regularly preached for about 15 minutes and the contrast in length, though not in the quality, between these two was such that some left the Dome after Newman's early sermons, however, he soon rebuilt the congregation.

Most worship in Methodism has always been conducted by local preachers. This does not seem to have been the case in Brighton and Hove. Nineteenth century Brighton and Hove was unusual in that the Bible Christian circuit never had more churches than ministers and so could have survived without local preachers. The only Primitive Methodist plan surviving from the first two decades of the twentieth century, that for the first quarter of 1913, shows that in the morning and evening services in these thirteen weeks for the three largest churches, only fourteen services out of a total of 78 possible occasions were taken by local preachers that is just under 18%. In contrast, the fourth church in Brighton and Hove, Portslade, only had its services, morning or evening, taken by a minister on three of the 26 possible occasions.

For the Wesleyans, from 1892 to 1920 Norfolk Road was a one church circuit so almost its services were taken by the minister. In the circuit covering all the other churches, in the morning and evening services in the 26 weeks from August 1902 to January, 1903, in the three largest churches, only seven services out of a total of 156 possible occasions were taken by local preachers, that is just over 4.5%. In the similar period from September, 2006 to February 2007, in the three largest churches 40 services out of a total of 142 possible occasions were taken by local preachers, that is just over 28%. In Brighton and Hove therefore overall local preachers play a far more prominent role in leading worship than they did one hundred years ago.

It is also worth noting that ministers take the services at the smaller churches far more frequently than they did a century ago.

"He is not a God of the dead, but of the living."
—Jesus.

"Life is a mission. Every other definition of life is false, and leads all who accept it astray."—MAZZINI.

"A sacred burden in this life ye bear,
Look on it, lift it, bear it solemnly;
Stand up and walk beneath it steadfastly;
Fail not for sorrow, falter not for sin,
But onward, upward, till the goal ye win."
—F. A. KEMBLE.

"I have finished my course . . . henceforth there is laid up for me a crown of righteousness, which the Lord, the righteous judge, shall give me."—PAUL.

Place and Time of Services.		JANUARY.				FEBRUARY.				MARCH.				APRIL.
		12	19	26		2	9	16	23	2	9	16	23	30	6
BRIGHTON.															
London Road Church.	11 6.45 8	Rose Rose Rose	Rose s Rose Rose	Rose Smith Rose		Rose Rose Rose	Rose s Rose Rose	Rose s Rose Rose	Rose Rose Rose	Rose s Rose Rose	Andrews Andrews Rose	Supply Supply Supply	Supply Supply Rose	Rose Taylor Rose	Rose Rose s Rose
Thursday	8														
Queen's Pk. Rd. Ch'ch	11 6.45	R. Smith Burton	R. Smith Rose	Smith Smith		Parsons Smith	Smith Galpin	Smith Newell	Smith Smith	Baker Merr'ld's	Smith Adams	Smith Smith	Smith Smith	Smith Taylor	Smith Smith
Tuesday		Smith	Smith	Smith		Smith	Smith	Smith			Smith	Smith			
Haywards Heath.	11 6.30 7.0	Merrif'ld R. Smith Baker	Wilton Dick'nsn Jones	Wilton Aldridge		Hilton s Honess Verrall	Aldridge Dalton Merrif'd	Newell Bales Dick'nsn	Newell Hilton†	Hilton Merr'ld's Cook	Supply Supply Bales	Supply Supply Bales	Jones Honess Merrif'd	Well'd s Welford Social
Wednesday															
Newhaven.	11 6.30	Andrews Andrews	Andrews Andrews	Andrews Andrews		Andrews Andw's S	Parsons Andrews	Andrews Burton	Andrews Andrews	Andrews Rose	Andrews Andw's S	Andrews Andrews	Taylor Taylor	Andrews Smith
Tuesday	7	Andrews	Andrews	Andrews		Andrews	Andrews	Higgins'n	Andrews	Andrews	Higgin'sn	Higgin'sn	Winder	Andrews
HOVE BRANCH.															
Goldstone Villas	11 7	Ford Taylor	Ford Ford	Funnell Ford		Ford s Ford s	Ford Parsons	Ford Ford	Ford s Ford s	Ford Burton	Ford Ford	Ford Ford	Ford Ford	Ford s Ford s
Wednesday	7.30	Ford	Ford	Ford		Ford	C.E.	Ford	Ford	Ford	Ford	Ford	Ford	Ford
Portslade	11 6.45	Awcock Ford s	R. Smith R. Smith	Awcock Ford		Waym'k Ford	Awcock Ford s	Waym'k Awcock	Ford s Ford s	Awcock Ford s	Awcock Ford s	Terry, sr. Burton	Awcock Awcock	Awcock Ford
Thursday	8.0	Ford	Ford	Waym'k		Ford	Awcock	Ford	Ford	Awcock	Ford	Parsons	Ford	Ford

Page from Primitive Methodist Plan, Jan-Apr 1913. It shows the dominance of the ministers at the larger churches – Rose at London Road: Smith at Queen's Park: Andrews at Newhaven and Ford at Goldstone Villas.

MORNING WORSHIP

The Wesleyan Methodist Conferences in the first half of the nineteenth century frequently reminded Methodists to follow the Liturgy of the Church of England, or John Wesley's abridgement of it, and published service books to that end. The frequency of the Conference urgings indicate that Wesleyan Methodism was moving away from that tradition. During the nineteenth century Wesleyan Methodism moved from the formal towards the informal, using the Anglican liturgy at the start of the century and moving towards the use of extempore prayer by the end of it. Congregations in large towns or cities were more likely to retain the liturgy. Norfolk Road started in 1869 by using Wesley's order of Morning Prayer and this continued, despite occasional attempts to change it, until at least the end of World War II.

Norfolk Road Wesleyan Methodist Church,
from a painting by E. Morris, 1910

Dorset Gardens was unusual in that it displayed a different tendency. As Sawyer noted in c. 1882, in the 1820s '[t]he Church of England form was not used' and worship consisted of 'singing, reading the Scriptures, and extemporary prayer, just as in Nonconformist Chapels today'. By the time he was writing he thought that: 'the service might be mistaken for that in an Episcopal Church.' However this was soon to change. By the 1890s there was a move at Dorset Gardens away from 'the liturgy'. There is no explicit evidence for this but the move may in part have been a reaction against the ritual found in the Anglo-Catholic churches in the area.

Both the Bible Christians and the Primitive Methodists produced service books in the nineteenth century but, as David Chapman points out in his recent study of the subject, *Born in Song*: 'these publications were more akin to manuals for ministers than a proper service book since ... no responses were expected from the congregation'. There is no evidence for either the Bible Christians or the Primitive Methodists in Brighton using any congregational service book.

The absence of service-books continued throughout much of the twentieth century although now they are much more likely to be used and Methodists have become used to giving the responses.

CHAPTER 8

The SPIRITUAL LIFE of the CHURCH - II

MUSIC

The musical tradition in Methodism consists of three main elements: congregational hymn-singing, the instrument(s) used to accompany that singing and choral music. Both John Wesley and successive Conferences of the various Connexions laid down regulations regarding each of these. Hymn-singing, according to Wesley's *Directions for Singing* in 1761, was to be done 'lustily' but 'modestly. Do not bawl ...', Methodists were instructed 'above all to sing spiritually'. Wesley disliked anthems and the 1787 Conference forbad their use as they could not be called 'joint worship'. In addition any form on 'concert' or 'performance', whether it be of 'sacred' or 'secular' music, was frowned on and the Wesleyan Conference in 1805 stated:

> 'Let no musical Festivals, or, as they are sometimes termed, Selections of Sacred Music, be either encouraged or permitted in any of our chapels ... under the pretence of getting money for charitable purposes.'

The same Conference also laid down that no musical instruments were to be used except a bass viol if the 'principal singer require it. The function of the principal singer was to give out the lines of the hymns. This was called 'lining'. The reason for lining was twofold, to save the cost of hymn-books and to overcome the problem of illiteracy. Lining made hymn-singing a slow business which is why Wesley recommended only two hymns in the service to keep it to his recommended length of one hour.

Methodists in Brighton may well have 'sung lustily' and certainly used lining for the first half of the nineteenth century as discussion in the Trustees' Minute Book for Dorset Gardens shows. However, for the rest they seem to have ignored the prohibitions. Almost from the beginning Dorset Gardens had an orchestra rather than just the bass viol. The reason for this is interesting and may be unique in Methodism.

The presence of George, Prince of Wales, at the Royal Pavilion had a major impact in at least one area of Methodist life. He was renowned for his love of music and had a fine orchestra. Some members of this orchestra were members at Dorset Gardens and played in the services there to lead the singing. The instruments included not only the bass viol but flute, French horn, double bass, bassoon, trombone, etc. Those who were in the King's private band would have had to leave just before eight o'clock to attend to their royal duties. The names of some these musicians, who were members at Dorset Gardens in the 1820s, such Gustavus Adolphus Bode and Charles Frederick William Mennich, imply a continental origin.

Consequently the standard of music at Dorset Gardens at that time must have been as high as in any Methodist church in the country. The withdrawal of the Court in the early period of Victoria's reign meant that the royal musicians also left and by the 1850s the orchestra at Dorset Gardens had been reduced to three. There was also the problem that the bass viol belonging to the Church could not be found!

A decision was taken, against the express and determined opposition of the Superintendent minister, the Rev. William B. Stephenson, to have an organ instead and a second-hand instrument was found and installed in 1855. The services celebrating its installation were conducted in the absence of the Superintendent minister! The Wesleyan newspaper, *The Watchman*, reported that it had been installed 'free of debt' and that during the celebrations presided over by the most junior minister, 'selections from the Messiah &c, were efficiently sung'. Whether a Superintendent minister would have allowed himself to be bypassed in this way before the disruption following the Conference of 1849 is open to question.

Following this a pattern emerged for Wesleyans in Brighton and Hove. On the building of a church a musical instrument would be installed to accompany the congregational singing. If it was a wealthy church, like Norfolk Road, this instrument would be a new organ from the outset. Less wealthy churches, acquired theirs second-hand from Wesleyan churches in the circuit who were upgrading their own organ. This happened in the 1890s to Southwick (from Norfolk Road) and Preston Park (from Dorset Gardens).

Although they probably started without any musical instrument in their various rooms, from the opening of Bristol Road in 1873 onwards each Bible Christian church started with an organ in place.

It is highly unlikely that the first Primitive Methodist church in the county, at Sussex Street in Brighton, had an organ when it was opened in 1856. The reports of the opening in the *Primitive Methodist Magazine*, written by the minister, mention the cost of the whole project and how people had saved a few pounds here and there but do not refer to an organ.

The Primitive Methodists in Brighton and Hove were not only the smallest and weakest financially of the three Connexions, they also spread themselves more thinly across more buildings. Consequently, with one exception, the first musical instrument in all their churches opened between 1874 and 1894 were harmoniums, the exception being Islingword Road which opened in 1881 with an organ for which William Dinnick was 'personally liable. All of these churches that survived to Methodist union in Brighton and Hove in 1934 had by that time bought an organ.

Of the three churches built after union Hollingbury has always had a piano. Patcham and Woodingdean each started with a piano and then bought an organ. In some churches pipe organs have been replaced by their computer/electronic equivalent as in Stanford Avenue and Dorset Gardens. However, Woodingdean moved from an electronic organ to a pipe organ in its new building opened in 1986. The guitar has also become a frequent accompaniment to the congregation.

Some organists have given a lifetime of service. Jimmy Hooker played for over 50 years at Dorset Gardens and the Dome and Lewis Holden has played for almost 70 years, first at Bristol Road, then at London Road, and is now on the rota at Stanford Avenue. Methodism remains incredibly indebted to men and women such as these.

All churches of all Connexions developed choirs, usually entirely voluntary. Norfolk Road at first had a professional robed choir but after 1884 relied on voluntary efforts, a move apparently caused by lack of harmony in the choir rather than in the music. No choir in the circuit is now robed. Choir practice has always been, and remains, a feature of church life and the repertoire has been extended greatly with a considerable international flavour. This does not just refer to Taizé chants which were probably first used regularly at Queen's Park in the 1980s, but to music from Africa, Asia and the Americas.

Many churches also had orchestras and youth bands, as at Stanford Avenue by 1911. The young people's orchestra at London Road played at the afternoon Bible class in the early years of the twentieth century. This tradition continues with Patcham having an adult and a junior orchestra each of which leads worship at various times during the year.

DEVELOPMENTS in WORSHIP

Methodist worship remains focussed where one hopes it has always been, on God: but clearly there have been many developments over the past two hundred years in the expression of that focus. Some liturgical practices have been adopted from other churches in the world-wide Methodist family. At baptism it is now common for a baby to be carried around the church to be shown to the people and the rubrics now provide for it. Apparently this practice is not recorded in Britain before the 1970s and seems to have come from the U.S.A. The Rev. Dr. R. John Tudor, Superintendent minister of Brighton (Dome Mission) circuit 1975-1980, introduced it here and he may have been one of the first ministers in Britain to do so. He also introduced the practice of standing for the presentation of the collection, now the normative use in the circuit.

Services for 'healing and wholeness' have also been introduced in Brighton and Hove. The Rev. Peter Shilling, Superintendent minister of the Brighton (Dome Mission) circuit 1986-1994 may have been the first to use them in the area. Their use was developed by the Rev. Doug Hopwood from his arrival in the Brighton & Hove circuit in 1992, and the Circuit Meeting adopted a statement on the matter in 2007.

Methodist attitudes towards quiet and meditation have changed greatly since the time when they would have been regarded as 'Catholic' practices. Prayer chants, such as those developed by Taizé have become common. Stanford Avenue has a 'meditation group' and has just opened a 'prayer garden … for quiet contemplation'. This features a sculpture designed by one of the church members, Sandra Battley, and is in memory of Dr Sandra Winn, a local preacher who died in 2006. The circuit also organises 'quiet days', most recently using the Benedictine monastery of Worth Abbey for this purpose.

The prayer garden at Stanford Avenue Methodist Church opened in 2006 in memory of local preacher, Dr. Sandra Winn.
(Methodist Recorder Photograph)

In addition many churches have a space set aside as a prayer chapel or a purpose built prayer chapel such as that at Dorset Gardens when it was opened in 2003.

Prayer Chapel at Dorset Gardens Methodist Church in 2007.

Members of the different Methodist Connexions and the different nonconformist groups in Brighton in the last half of the nineteenth century attended the opening of each other's buildings, shared in each other's celebrations and joined in the funerals of their respective ministers and leading layfolk. But there are very few references before 1914 to the participation in such events of leading representatives of the Church of England.

There was a great change after World War I and clergy of the Church of England, including bishops, would take part in Methodist events. At the Dome on the evening of Monday, 3 October, 1932 there was a great celebration to celebrate Methodist Union. Four hymns were sung, three of them by Charles Wesley. Greetings were brought from the county representatives of the major nonconformist churches and from the Vicar of Brighton. The final address, which was preceded by 'O for a thousand tongues to sing' and followed by 'the Hallelujah Chorus', was given by the Rt. Rev. Bishop Whitehead, late Bishop of Madras. The idea of inviting an Anglican bishop to give the concluding address at such an event shows how far in the improvement in relations between the churches had come in a few decades.

The Liturgical Movement referred to in the last chapter clearly had a major impact on worship in Methodism as well as in other Churches. Many of the changes in Methodist practice in Brighton and Hove outlined in this chapter such as the increased eucharistic practice are examples of this. Although it is not the same as the Ecumenical Movement there are clearly both similarities and interconnections. The relations between the different Churches in Brighton and Hove has improved greatly especially since Vatican II (1962-1965).

Methodists are involved in the various groups of 'Churches Together …' in Brighton and Hove and ministers join in fraternals. There is often very close working together both in worship and in other activities. At Woodingdean once a month the evening service is shared with the local Anglicans using their respective churches alternately.

Woodingdean Methodist Church in 2007.

In her history of Patcham Methodist Church Nanette Buck records the time when they had to leave their building (called the 'Barn') on a temporary basis in 1967:

> 'As the Barn doors closed a new door opened. An invitation was received from the Roman Catholic Church of St. Thomas More for the congregation to have free use of their building on Sunday evenings until the new church was opened. This fine act of Christian unity was gratefully accepted and for the next 18 months evening services were held at St. Thomas More Church ... Father Vann and his flock were to prove excellent friends to the Methodists during their days of homelessness. Their final gracious act was to give the metal cross which forms the centre of the Celtic cross in the sanctuary.'

Such a sharing would have been unthinkable fifty years earlier let alone in the nineteenth century.

Developments in technology have also been used in the churches and the building of a new church at Dorset Gardens in 2003 enabled that society in 2006, under the guidance of one of its younger members, Alexander Harrington, to install computerised equipment in the church to enable the words of the hymns and readings, amongst many other uses, to be displayed during worship. Such facilities mean that some preachers now enhance their sermon with the use of video or DVD. A further development is that of the 'Fresh Expressions' movement. In 2005 Dorset Gardens started a Café Connexion once a month in the evening which is an informal café-style service and which attracts those looking for alternative forms of worship.

The first Methodist Empire radio broadcast service in the country was that from London Road on 18 March, 1934. The minister, the Rev. William H. Holtby, later received letters appreciation from as far afield as Nigeria and South Africa. Since that time a number of services have been broadcast both on radio and television.

If, and it is only one criterion among many, the numbers of members of a circuit who become ministers or deaconesses (no one from the circuit has yet offered for the diaconate) is a sign of the spiritual health of the community, then the most recent fifty years of the past two hundred would indicate that Methodism in Brighton and Hove is now at its greatest spiritual strength.

	Ordained as Ministers	**Ordained as Wesley Deaconesses**
1807-1856	0	Did not yet exist
1857-1906	5	3 (all working as local 'sisters')
1907-1956	4	2
1957-2006	9	3 (order closed to recruitment 1978)

The most recent are:

Ministers

Keith Bamford
Neil Bartlett
Gary Homewood
Heather Leake (now Leake Date)
Peter Mooring
Patricia (Pat) Percival
Harvey Richardson
Jean Simmonds
David Wheeler

Deaconesses

Audrey Deane
Joan Farrow
Brenda Fletcher

CHAPTER 9

The CHURCH and its YOUNG PEOPLE

Within a year of the Wesleyan Methodists building Dorset Gardens in 1808 they had started a Sunday school which met first in the gallery. The alterations to Dorset Gardens in the 1820s meant that the Sunday school was given a special hall over the vestry. In 1826 the church acquired a room at the top of nearby Carlton Hill which was used as a day school during the week, the idea being to use it as a 'Mission Sunday school'. On Sundays there was a Sunday school with an occasional evening service for adults.

Nelson Row Wesleyan Methodist Sunday School and Mission Hall in about 1904.

With at least 300 children this building proved to be inadequate and in 1834 they laid the foundation stones for a new building in Nelson Row, a few hundred yards to the northwest of Dorset Gardens and one of the poorest areas of Brighton. This was opened in 1835 but in turn proved to be too small and another floor for girls was added in 1836. The two rooms were connected by two hatches in the floor of the upper story so that the superintendent could stand in the pulpit and speak to both the boys and the girls at once. A further floor was added in 1850 to cater for the "infants". Nelson Row also had a Wesleyan Day school which by 1845 had 120 pupils but for which no records survive.

We need to recall that the Sunday school in the nineteenth century had a different function compared to today. Before the advent of state education in 1870 most children learnt the basics of reading and writing in Sunday schools, a movement that had been started in the late eighteenth century. There was much debate within early nineteenth century Methodism about whether to teach writing on Sundays and how much secular education, if any, should be allowed. The Report of the Brighton Wesleyan Sunday school Committee in 1853 supported secular education in its schools but wanted: 'Religion mingled with everything so that every item of secular knowledge they acquire, may be consecrated by the feelings & hopes of true religion.'

There is much debate about how far the Sunday schools were run by the middle-class for the poor, or were a working-class movement. By the 1850s Dorset Gardens ran two Sunday schools, one at Dorset Gardens, the other at Nelson Row. It must be assumed that the former were for the children of members and the latter a mission to the poorer elements of the town. However, there was concern at Dorset Gardens that many of the children of members did not attend the Sunday school. In the 1850s the syllabus included teaching the Wesleyan catechism and ensuring that the children at Dorset

Gardens knew the proper responses for morning prayer. One of the wealthier members gave prayer books for this purpose.

However, there were many problems. In 1850 a report to the Brighton Wesleyan Sunday School Committee commented that the attendance of teachers at the Windsor Street Sunday School was 'exceedingly unfavourable' and by 1854 'the school was almost broken up'. One of the reasons for this lay in the disruption within Wesleyan Methodism with a number of the Sunday school teachers taking the side of the 'reformers' and being expelled from the Wesleyan membership.

A further problem at this time was that a local Church of England day school would not allow children to attend unless they also went to that Church's Sunday school. This had a major impact on numbers at Nelson Row. For reasons which are not fully clear, throughout the first half of the nineteenth century Sussex had one of the lowest percentages of the population being enrolled in Sunday schools of all types.

The decline in fortunes of all Methodist Connexions in Brighton and Hove in the 1850s and 1860s was mirrored in the Sunday schools. For all churches both locally and nationally attendance at Sunday school did not translate into church membership. As Philip Cliff commented in his history of the movement "being 'sent' was not the same as "being 'taken'".

This is a point worth emphasising. In her study of Methodist Sunday schools in nineteenth century Sussex Jacqueline Brown includes the table of membership in the Report of the Brighton Sunday School Union of 1871. This gives 22 schools, most of them not Methodist. These had 3,955 scholars on their books, excluding infants. The final column is 'scholars joining church'. The grand total for that year is 25! Within these figures the Methodist statistics for the three connexions are 720 scholars with a total of four joining the various churches! Even given the fact that the great surge under Dinnick, Martin and Westerdale had yet to come and state education had not yet got under way, these figures should be a salutary reminder not to confuse eager attendance at Sunday school with willingness to join the relevant Church.

In line with a national change the reinvigoration in Brighton began to occur in the 1870s and continued for the rest of the century and beyond. By the time of the centenary celebrations in 1909 the Wesleyan Sunday schools were flourishing and being commended for using the latest teaching techniques. However, the translation from Sunday school membership to church membership remained more elusive than the churches wanted or expected.

The Sunday school Anniversary had been a feature of Sunday school life almost from the beginning. At first the children and their teachers paraded around the town with banners (which were 'the inspiration for later Trade Union banners'). The children were then taken to a nearby park and given refreshments. By the turn of the century this had turned into a full day out. For example in July each year in the 1890s the London Road Primitive Methodist Church took the pupils and teachers to Poynings by charabanc.

One of the impacts of World War I was a decline in attendance at Sunday schools, as many teachers were no longer available. This decline across all denominations was noted at a meeting in 1916, which reached no definite conclusions other than noting that there were 'other attractions' and 'that it was wartime'. There were other problems as well. The Primitive Methodist Lay Worker at Goldstone Villas in 1908, Thomas Heywood, recalled that at one point the older boys carried the Sunday school superintendent outside and dumped him 'quite gently ... and told him not to come back'. Poor behaviour occurred elsewhere. In 1904 there was concern about the 'use of catapults' by boys in the gallery during the long prayer at Hove.

All Methodist churches had Sunday schools. Until the middle of the twentieth century they usually met in the afternoon but gradually the change in family life styles led to meeting in the morning as at Patcham from 1962. In the next decade there was a move to rename it as 'Junior Church' in order to distance itself from the concept of 'school'. Stanford Avenue made this change in 1973. Until their new church had been opened in 1986 Woodingdean kept the afternoon Sunday school because their multi-purpose hall could not deal with concurrent activities.

The Sunday school was not the only means by which churches attempted to attract and retain young people. Some activities were local in scope. Norfolk Road had a festival for young people called 'the crowning of the May Queen' which included as many as possible of all the young people connected with the church in any way and, as Dorothy Patching recalls, involved many rehearsals and a pageant with singing and playlets. This annual ceremony at Norfolk Road lasted until the church closed in 1964.

There were two main national uniformed organisations. The Boys' and Girls' Brigades, and the Scout and Guide movements. The former were founded in 1883 with the Girls sections in the first years of the twentieth century. The Scouts and Guides stem from later in the first decade of the twentieth century.

The various churches first formed Boys' Brigades, followed in each case by the Girls' equivalent. The first Boys' Brigade and Girls' Guildry companies in Brighton were started by the Wesleyans at Norfolk Road followed soon after by the Bible Christians at Bristol Road whose company, later famous as the 'Dandy Fifth', was formed in 1898. They were followed by all the other churches of their respective Connexions. The Primitive Methodists seem to have been the least enthusiastic in the early years, London Road even formed a 'Natural History Group' in the 1900s 'to retain boys who were being captured by the Boys' Brigade.'

The Scout and Guide movement started later and tended to be found more in Brighton and Hove in Wesleyan Methodist churches. The Scout Troop at Dorset Gardens (now called the 14th Brighton) is still going strong, having survived the enforced break with the building whilst it was being built anew. This Troop had been formed in 1923 as an offshoot of the Troop of its fellow Wesleyan Methodist church, Preston Park. After Preston Park was bombed in 1943 its Troop (the 7th Brighton) joined Stanford Avenue.

Besides those mentioned above there are currently Guides, Brownies or Rainbow groups at Hollingbury and Woodingdean, and Beavers, Cubs and Girls' Brigade at Patcham.

The reason for the initial lack of enthusiasm by the Primitive Methodists may have been because they were committed to the 'Band of Hope'. This was a national organisation founded in 1847 and dedicated to the promotion of total abstinence. Although a number of churches of all Methodist connexions in Brighton and Hove had Bands of Hope, it was strongest at Queen's Park which always took part in the annual Pageant at the Dome in the 1920s and 1930s where the 'Temperance Queen' was crowned. However, by the 1950s the movement was in decline. Not all churches had Bands of Hope. In the years after World War I Hove decided not to have a Band of Hope or to restart its Wesley Guild in order to focus on its 'existing commitments to young people's work', but the Hove Wesley Guild had re-started by 1930.

Band of Hope Demonstration, Brighton 1923.

There was a move to more physical activities during the twentieth century. The Rev. Alec Sidebottom who became minister at Bristol Road in 1939 was very keen on sport and a qualified football referee. Under his leadership as chaplain of the 'Dandy Fifth' Boys' Brigade 'football now took the place of drill' and the company was very successful in football competitions. The involvement with sport developed and after World War II and into the 1950s the Brighton and Hove circuit had its own athletics championships with two divisions of teams.

Sport was also an aspect of the Methodist Association of Youth Clubs, MAYC, which was founded in 1945. For example in the Brighton and Hove circuit, Hove, Patcham and Stanford Avenue established Youth Clubs under the MAYC banner and took part in competitions involving 5-a-side football, netball and table tennis, with finals at the MAYC weekend at the Albert Hall in London. These weekends also included displays which focussed on various areas of Christian faith. Hove joined other clubs in 1966 in the "Final Item" of the display to bring the show to a climax with a Bible based demonstration.

Apart from the uniformed organisations, since the 1950s there has been a greater focus on the opportunities given through the church for drama and music, especially when the whole church community is involved, such as the production of *Joseph and his Amazing Technicolor Dreamcoat* at Hove in 1989. In 2005, a young people's circuit performing arts group based at Hollingbury gave a dramatic presentation at Patcham.

A further development has been the introduction of 'holiday clubs' and weekly 'after school clubs' for local children. Churches such as Dorset Gardens and Patcham provide both the space and the personnel to look after many children (about 200 at Patcham in 2006) for a week or so during school holidays. As in so much of current Methodist life this is seen as a way of serving the community and all children regardless of religious affiliation are welcome.

One of the changes in work with young people has been brought about by legislation concerning child protection. Led by the Superintendent minister, the Rev. Kathleen Allen, and the Circuit Safeguarding Officer, Maggie Wheeler of Patcham, (now succeeded by Anne Walker of Stanford Avenue), the circuit set up a 'Circuit Taking Care Group' which assists each church in the circuit to continue to take its responsibilities very seriously indeed.

Over the past two hundred years from the first Methodist Sunday School in 1809 to the present Methodists have been committed to working with and engaging with young people, hopefully realising that they too were young once.

CHAPTER 10

LEADERSHIP in the CHURCH

MINISTERS and DEACONESSES

For most of the nineteenth century most ministers received no college training although they were expected to study. The Rev. Dr. George Osborn, one of the leaders of Wesleyan Methodism in the last half of the nineteenth century, wrote of his early ministry in the Brighton circuit in 1829 that, living in Worthing, "being free from some distractions incident to the larger place [Brighton]. I greatly enjoyed my opportunities of reading and study."

In the early part of the nineteenth century Brighton was clearly a good place for ministerial self-improvement as the Rev. Joseph Sutcliffe, one of the leading biblical scholars in Wesleyan Methodism, completed his two-volume Bible commentary whilst stationed in Brighton in 1834. Such study was not confined to the Wesleyan tradition. The Rev. James Way, a Bible Christian minister stationed in Brighton in 1831-1832, heard of a copy of Clarke's nine-volume Bible commentary for sale at half price in Tenterden in Kent. The price was over half his annual stipend but he walked the forty miles to Tenterden, bought the books and walked back carrying the large volumes.

Training for the Methodist ministry varied greatly within the three connexions in Brighton and Hove. The Wesleyan Methodists opened their first such institution in 1835, the Primitive Methodists in 1865 and the Bible Christians never had one, although after 1907 prospective ministers may have gone to the United Methodist college. The fact that the Wesleyans and the Primitive Methodists had colleges from these dates does not mean that all or even most ministers attended them from that time. In addition we need to recall that non-Anglicans could not receive degrees from Oxford or Cambridge until 1871.

In the years before Methodist union there were several Wesleyan ministers who had obtained a degree, the Rev. Hugh Price Hughes (1872-1875) among them. Some of these, like the Rev. Dr. Joseph Finnemore (1891-1894), had doctorates. However, it was not until 1926 that a Primitive Methodist minister with a degree was appointed, and no Bible Christian or United Methodist minister in Brighton had a degree.

A lack of academic degree should not be understood at all as a lack of training to become a minister and Primitive Methodism, in particular, was proud of the intellectual rigour of its ministerial training at Hartley College under the famous A. S. Peake who was there from 1892 to his death in 1929.

In the nineteenth century Brighton seems to have been used by all the Connexions as an 'easy' circuit in which they could place ministers in need of a rest. We have already seen that the Bible Christian Conference sent the Rev. Jehu Martin to Brighton in 1870 because he was regarded as being 'enfeebled' by illness. In 1818 the Wesleyan Conference sent the Rev. John Smith from Durham to Brighton for his health. In 1824 the Rev. William Shrewsbury had to flee for his life from Barbados where he was being persecuted by those upholding slavery. Arriving in England in June of that year he was stationed by the Wesleyan Conference in Brighton in order to recover. Shrewsbury called it 'a comfortable circuit' and found himself 'amongst a very kind and loving people.'

All ministers lived in rented property for much of the nineteenth century and probationer ministers still used rented accommodation into the 1950s. The provision of manses began in the last part of the nineteenth century. This could cause problems. The Rev. Joseph Dixon arrived in 1897 to take up the Wesleyan superintendency only to discover that the 'preacher's house has been given up' and that his first task 'was to go house-hunting'.

Rent, travel and washing was paid for by the circuit, together with the medical bills. This last could be a large amount. In 1813 the medical bill for the Wesleyan circuit totalled just over £14 which was over 40% of the total stipend given to the minister and his wife for that year. Wesleyan Methodist ministers received allowances for children and a servant, the Primitive Methodist ministers received them only for children.

The stipends themselves, which were laid down by the various Conferences, were low in the first half of the nineteenth century. In 1824 the Wesleyan Superintendent was given 16 guineas a year as was his wife, whose money was given first. This total of £33 12s dwarfed that of the first Bible Christian Superintendent minister who received just £12 p.a. which was well below the wage of an agricultural labourer. For example, in 1834 the 'Tolpuddle Martyrs', agricultural labourers in Dorset most of whom were Wesleyan Methodists, formed a friendly society to protest at a reduction in wages to just over £15 p.a. This is not fully comparable as the minister did have many of his expenses, such as accommodation, paid for.

The Primitive Methodists were also sparing. The Superintendent ministers in 1850 received just over £31 p.a. but the probationer minister received just £14 p.a. although his rent and food were paid for. George Osborn, as a Wesleyan probationer minister in Brighton in 1829, worked out that he received, including all expenses, just under £28 p.a. on which he commented that: 'it is not wonderful to find that this was occasionally supplemented from "home".'

Comparing clerical incomes is notoriously difficult but it is clear that, in the first half of the nineteenth century, Methodist ministers in all connexions were given stipends far below that of clergymen of the Church of England when the average stipend for a curate in 1837 was £81 p.a.

Gradually stipends were increased during the nineteenth century. By 1859 a married Wesleyan Methodist minister was receiving £117 p.a. although a Primitive Methodist minister in a similar situation received half as much and a Bible Christian minister even less, the Rev. William Beer's stipend was 'increased' to £42 p.a. in 1864!

The increasing membership in the last quarter of the nineteenth century, much of it due to the unstinting efforts of ministers like Martin for the Bible Christians and Dinnick for the Primitive Methodists, led their respective circuits to increase their stipends. In 1888 Dinnick's stipend was increased from £100 p.a. to £140 p.a. and in 1889 the Bible Christians increased the stipend from £80 p.a. to £100 p.a. It should be noted that in each case this was above the connexional norm. In the case of the Primitive Methodists it was well above as in 1893 the stipend nationally was still only £88 p.a.

By the 1920s the stipends of the three Methodist connexions which would eventually unite to become the Methodist Church were very similar, with most ministers receiving a stipend of £240 p.a. and Superintendents an extra allowance of £20 or £30 p.a. All ministers received extra allowances for their children.

For most of the nineteenth century ministers in all three connexions stayed for one, two or three years. The Wesleyans were most rigorous in their application of the three-year maximum period and we have already seen the problems that the Rev. Frank Ballard caused in 1894 when he wanted to extend his appointment at the Brighton (Norfolk Road) circuit beyond those three years. Two of Ballard's successors at Norfolk Road were stationed for more than three years, including the Rev. E. Aldom French (1904-1910) who founded the Dome Mission at the beginning of his fourth year. Without the change brought about by Ballard the Dome Mission would probably never have begun.

The Rev. E. Aldom French (in 1904)
Wesleyan Methodist Superintendent minister
Brighton (Norfolk Road) circuit, 1904-1910.
Founder of the Dome Mission.

The first Wesleyan appointment for more than six years was at Dorset Gardens which had by this time taken responsibility for the Dome Mission and where the Rev. J. Morris Bold was minister from 1921 to 1928 when his departure was forced by the ill-health of his wife. The ministers at Dorset Gardens, which was the Brighton (Dome Mission) circuit from 1934, often had long tenures. The longest was that of the Rev. Dr. Leslie Newman who was stationed there from 1953 to his retirement in 1967.

However, the Rev. Doug Hopwood served for even longer being a minister here from 1992 to his retirement in 2007. He was the superintendent minister of the Brighton & Hove circuit until the formation of the new Brighton and Hove circuit in

1997, when the area had its first woman superintendent minister, the Rev. Mary Bailey.

One of the quirks of ministerial appointments arose during World War I. Possibly the most famous ministers nationally in late nineteenth century and early twentieth century Methodism (of all connexions) were the Rev. Hugh Price Hughes (1847-1902) and the Rev. Dr John Scott Lidgett (1854-1953), who was called *'Archbishop of Methodism?'* in the title of a recent biography. Because ministers were leaving circuit work to become military chaplains some senior ministers took on more than one superintendency but this may have been purely nominal. For example according to the 1916 Minutes of the Wesleyan Conference, Lidgett, the Chair of the District, was appointed as Superintendent to both Brighton circuits, as well as retaining his appointments in London. It is possible that at least one of these was a misprint as *Hall's Circuits and Ministers 1913-1923* only gives Lidgett at the Brighton (Norfolk Road) circuit. The Rev. Joseph Dixon was superintendent of the Brighton (Dorset Gardens) circuit from 1914 to 1917. Lidgett may well never have acted as Superintendent at Norfolk Road but as it stands the record means that Norfolk Road Wesleyan Methodist Church has a unique place in Methodism as being the only church in the country to count both the Rev. Hugh Price Hughes and the Rev. Dr. John Scott Lidgett among its past ministers.

Until Martin's arrival in 1870 most Bible Christian ministers were stationed for one year only, although by 1870 two-year appointments were becoming more common. Writing in c. 1882 Sawyer noted that the Bible Christians in Brighton had petitioned the Conference most strongly for a more permanent minister and consequently Martin was appointed, by special arrangement of the Conference, for eight years. Martin's great success in revitalising the society and building a new church confirmed the decision to make an exception. After a few three-year appointments there then came the appointment of the Rev. Samuel Brown Lane, which lasted for almost nineteen years, from 1893 until his death in 1912.

This length of appointment was eclipsed by the Rev. William Dinnick who was stationed in Brighton by the Primitive Methodists for twenty-five years, from 1876 until his death in 1901. Previously the length of ministry in Brighton and Hove for Primitive Methodist ministers had been similar to the Bible Christians, but following Dinnick there were a number of long ministries including that of the Rev. William Hammond, who was minister from 1915 to 1926. In 1918 he was elected President of the Primitive Methodist Conference. Whilst a number of ministers stationed in Brighton and Hove had been, or went on to be, the Presidents of their respective Conferences, the only other connexional Presidency bestowed on a minister then serving in Brighton and Hove was that of the Rev. Samuel Brown Lane, who was President of the Bible Christian Conference for 1905-1906.

Almost 450 ministers have served in Brighton and Hove over the past two hundred years, bringing a vast range of talents and skills. Almost all have been men. The first woman to be appointed in the twentieth century was the Rev. Mary Bailey who was appointed as Superintendent of the Brighton (Dome Mission) circuit in 1994 and became the first Superintendent of the new joint Brighton & Hove circuit to be succeeded, by the time of publication, by two other women as Superintendents. However, the Bible Christians did station women ministers in Brighton in the very early years, although Griffin in his otherwise excellent history mistakenly calls them 'deaconess'. The last to be stationed in the Chichester and Brighton Mission was Amy Terry from 1838 to 1839. Of the over 260 whose birthplace is known the greatest concentration come from the Methodist strongholds of Cornwall (29), Devon (26), Yorkshire (25) and Lancashire (22). Sussex provides hardly any!

The Wesley Deaconess Order was founded in 1890. The first Wesley Deaconess to be appointed to Brighton was Emma Johnson who was based at Dorset Gardens between 1909 and 1912. There was then a gap for the war years, then from 1921 for sixty years until 1981 a Deaconess was appointed to Brighton to work in the Dome Mission.

However, these were not the only Deaconesses to work in the Wesleyan Methodist Church in Brighton. In 1897 a member at Dorset Gardens, Clara Attrill, offered her services to the Church as a 'sister' and was accepted to start on 1 May of that year. She worked until 1908 when she was compelled to resign through ill-health having been told by her doctor to take absolute rest for one year! She was replaced by Sister Emma Johnson, who served until 1912 when she left Dorset Gardens to go to the Dome Mission, at that point under Norfolk Road. Norfolk Road had already, like Dorset Gardens, been using its 'own' deaconesses before applying to the Wesley Deaconess Order.

The last Wesley Deaconess to serve at the Dome Mission was Sister Joyce Rawkins who left in 1981, having reached the maximum permitted term of ten years. The Wesley Deaconess Order had ceased recruiting in 1978 and the Brighton (Dome Mission) circuit decided not to replace Sister Joyce, proving what had been thought for years that she was, in Len Wright's words, 'irreplaceable'.

The devoted work of these deaconesses, often behind the scenes and little sung, should not go unnoticed and unrecorded and will undoubtedly receive greater mention in the specific history of Dorset Gardens which celebrates its own bicentenary in 2008.

The LAITY

Methodism has always relied immensely on its laity. In Brighton and Hove this is especially true as the origins of Wesleyan Methodism lay in the prayer meetings of soldiers who were joined by some local people. It was these local people, amongst whom the name of Edward Beves stands first, who asked for a minister to be sent. As we saw in Chapter 3, both the first Bible Christian and Primitive Methodists ministers were invited to Brighton by people already in the town. The same pattern was followed by the small and short-lived United Methodist Free Church which in 1861 requested their Conference to send a resident minister.

So all Methodist connexions in Brighton and Hove began with a very small group of layfolk asking for a minister to be sent. They did not start with the arrival of a minister who preached and found a hearing.

It would be impossible to mention the vast number of those who have made such a contribution to Methodism in Brighton and Hove. Some names have already been referred to in specific instances but here we need to look at just a few who have made a significant contribution.

The first surname must be that of Beves. Edward Beves should be accounted the effective founder of Methodism in Brighton. His sons all followed him as office-holders in the circuit and at Dorset Gardens, indeed at least one meeting of the trustees of Dorset Gardens in 1855 consisted entirely of members of the family. In the period 1827 to 1872 of the 565 known attendances of the Dorset Gardens Trust by ministers and laity, almost 47% were by members of the Beves family. This tradition of service continued into the third generation with Edward Beves' grandson, also Edward, being a major figure at Norfolk Road until he died in 1913.

One of the leading nineteenth century Bible Christian layman was George Humphreys who not only held offices within the church, circuit and connexion, but played cricket for Sussex and represented the Bible Christians, together with the then minister in Brighton, the Rev. John H. Batt, at the Methodist Ecumenical Conference in Washington, U.S.A. in 1891.

Walter Gillett also held church, circuit and connexional office for the Bible Christians and was sufficiently highly regarded to be one of the people in *'Biographical Sketches of Bible Christians'* by William Mitchell in 1906.

Walter Gillett, leading Bible Christian layman, 1906. Printer and Stationer.

The leading Primitive Methodist layman of the nineteenth century was undoubtedly Edward Lowther, after whom Lowther Road in Brighton is named. He had come to Brighton from Northumberland having worked in the coalmines as a boy, in a seam less than 2 feet high, and had built up a coal merchant's business in Brighton, becoming a Councillor, Alderman and J.P. He held all the major offices in the church and circuit and was one of William Dinnick's main supporters.

EDWARD LOWTHER,

Alderman Edward Lowther JP, c. 1910. Coal-merchant: Primitive Methodist circuit steward.

The same devotion can be seen after Methodist union. In the Dome Mission circuit there was Ernest Ovenden, the father of Grace Ovenden who will be mentioned later. He held all the major offices at the Dome for very many years 'strove unceasingly for the completion of' Woodingdean Church when 'several times it could so easily have been lost'.

Ron Ivens died in 1953. As a member of Norfolk Road he had been indefatigable in the years immediately following the end of World War I in getting the Dome Mission reinstated, despite the opposition of his superintendent minister. He was also to make, what Nanette Buck in her history of Patcham termed, 'an outstanding contribution to the establishment of the Patcham church'. His portrait was hung in the Patcham vestry.

A conscious decision has been taken to avoid mentioning here any of those now living being fully aware that a great mass of work in Methodism is done by the laity without whom there would be no church at all. To mention one really means mentioning all and that would be impossible. We should all be deeply grateful for the countless unsung people who have tried to bring the 'life of Christ' to life in their own lives and so affect the lives of others.

CHAPTER 11

LIFE in the CHURCH

In the nineteenth century Methodism, together with Baptist, Congregational and similar denominations, became part of the Nonconformist tradition and of what has become known as the 'chapel' or 'Nonconformist' culture. This reached its heyday in the last half of the nineteenth century and first decades of the twentieth. Most students of 'chapel culture' like Munson and Young or of English nonconformity, like Binfield, Brown, Johnson, and Shaw and Kreider, finish their studies by 1950 or earlier.

Put simply, in the period 1880-1914 a member of a Methodist church in Brighton and Hove could find in their church all that was needed for spiritual activity, entertainment, fellowship, education, economic and social well-being, political involvement, etc. The relationship with the wider society will be dealt with in the next chapter. Here we will look at 'life within the church community'.

In 1900 a family might read the weekly Church newspaper and take the monthly connexional magazine, with a special magazine for the children. On Sunday the whole family would attend worship in the morning, the children go to Sunday School in the afternoon and their parents to an activity such as a 'Pleasant Sunday Afternoon'. The family would then attend evening worship. During the week there would be class or prayer meetings and a variety of other activities. The Wesleyans had the 'Wesley Guild', the Hove group met on Monday evenings between 8.15 and 9.30. The Primitive Methodists and Bible Christians had 'Christian Endeavour', the Bristol Road group met on Tuesdays at 8.30. In addition to Sunday school there were the Boys' Brigade and Girls' Guildry for the children. In 1894 the trustees at Dorset Gardens agreed to have a gymnasium 'for the benefit of the elder scholars' but forbad boxing. The whole family might attend choir practice or join a band or orchestra and take part in the regular concerts.

In 1900 there was no 'welfare state'. Old Age Pension for those aged 70 or over was only introduced in 1908 and National Insurance in 1911. Before this time there was no national scheme to assist those who were old, sick, or unemployed. People who were too poor or ill had had few recourses outside the workhouse. The current Brighton General hospital is on the site of the main workhouse in Brighton which it took over in 1935. One of the ways that people could obtain help in need was through membership of a Friendly Society or a group such as a Trades Union. Churches tried to fill the gap into which many fell. Methodists had always used their collection for the needy given at Holy Communion. These monies were known as the 'Poor Fund'.

In the period 1880-1914 the Leaders' Meetings of Methodist churches might meet as often as once a month. A major part of their business was in determining who to help from the 'Poor Fund'. Those helped were usually given cash although a gift of coal might also be included, sometimes the money might be given each week for a quarter.

In order to help people save on a regular basis most churches established a 'slate club'. That at London Road started in 1911 and only closed in 1972, over 1,100 people had been members at one point or another, a far larger figure than the membership of the Church. This discrepancy is a aspect of church life that will be referred to later.

Whilst it is true that the all-encompassing chapel culture of the period 1880-1914 has disappeared the range of activities offered within the church were expanded in the inter-war period and by 1950 there was a far greater variety. For example, as has been mentioned, in the years immediately after World War II the Brighton and Hove circuit organised an annual Sports Day for its young people with promotion and demotion from the two divisions of the League. Well over 100 young people would take part and receive the certificates awarded. Such events had disappeared by the 1960s with the decrease in large numbers at Sunday schools and the increased family leisure activity.

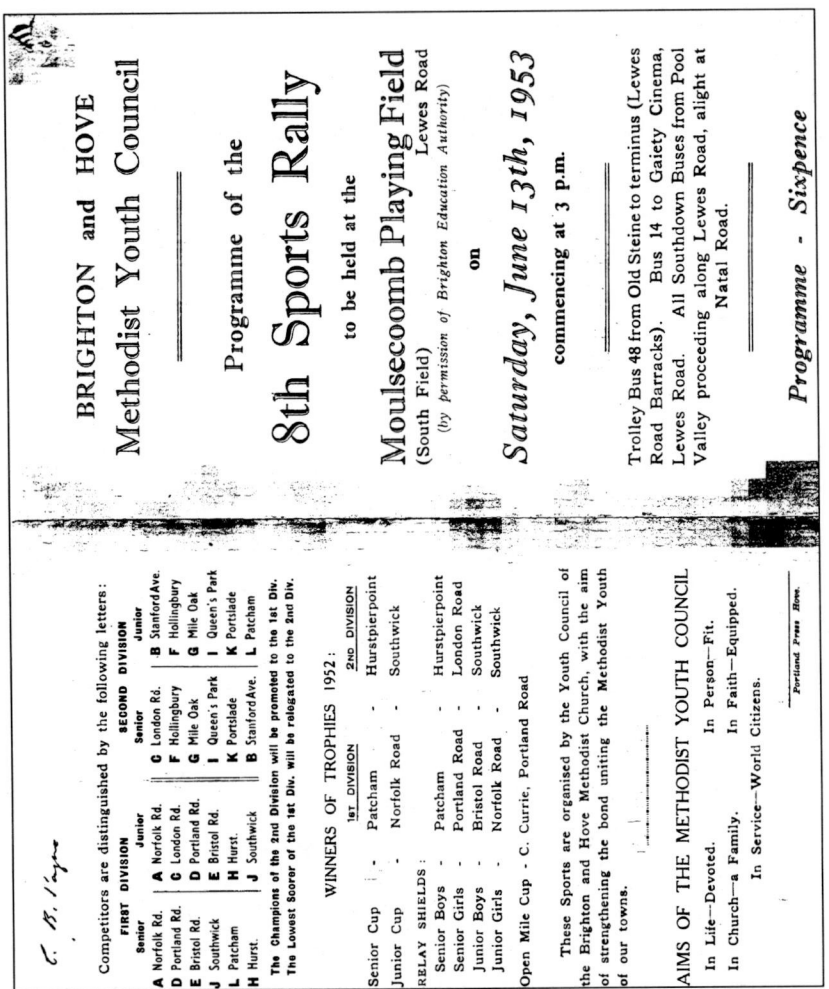

Programme for Brighton & Hove Circuit 8th Sports Day, 1953

Dramatic performances were also a feature of many of the churches and the church buildings had rooms with stages and all that was necessary for such performances. Preston Park and Stanford Avenue each had active dramatic societies before the start of World War II and these combined when Preston Park had to merge with Stanford Avenue following the destruction of their premises in 1943. They are now called 'the Stanford Players' and put on productions like *'Mother Goose'* (1997). Hove performed plays such as *'Miracle'* and Easter Passion plays and the 'Barnstormers' of Patcham produced Cole Porter's *'Anything Goes'* (2007).

This enthusiasm for drama was developed and a Brighton and Hove Methodist Drama Group was formed. In 1991 they put on a performance of the 'Passion' from the Tony Harrison's trilogy *'the Mysteries'* based on medieval mystery plays and produced by Hove member, Bob Hinton. This was so popular that it was performed at nine different venues as well as having three performances as part of the 1992 Brighton Festival. It was followed in 1999 and 2000, as part of the Millennium celebrations, by *'Nativity'* from the same trilogy.

Dorset Gardens, being so much part of the centre of Brighton, has used its new building to house a number of events associated with the Brighton Festival. From *'Faith in the City'* in 2004 there has been an art exhibition each year in conjunction with the Festival. Artistic activity has not been confined to the Festival and, led by Shirley Veater, there have been art classes and exhibitions in the church on themes such as *'Brighton Beautiful'* in August 2006. Membership of these classes is not confined to members of the church and in 2007 there 40 members of the 'Art & Craft Club'.

Literature in general has also been an important aspect of church life over the past two hundred years although that has not always been so. One of John Wesley's preachers, John Pawson, burnt Wesley's annotated copy of Shakespeare which he considered 'unedifying' and 'worthless lumber'. This was completely against the tenor of Wesley's life. In his recent study of Wesley, John Munsey Turner points out that Wesley 'can be seen as a 'compulsive educator'. Wesley wanted Methodists to read and edited for their edification a 50 volume *Christian Library* of what he considered important works, from a wide range of writers including the early Church Fathers as well as Anglican, Roman Catholic and Puritan writers.

In the nineteenth century the Superintendent minister of each Connexion was supposed to keep a stock of books and magazines and to act as an agent for their respective 'book room'. Only one inventory survives, that for the Wesleyan circuit for August 1826 when the departing minister, the Rev. Jonathan Barker, left detailed instructions for his successor. Apart from a variety of Magazines and Hymn Books he had collections of Benson's Sermons and one of Clarke's commentaries on Hosea in stock.

The Wesley Guild was started nationally in 1896 as a youth movement. At Hove one meeting in four was devoted to 'literary' activities such as a lecture on 'Hamlet' given by the minister the Rev. Ernest J. B. Kirtlan in May 1910. Other meetings were both devotional and educational as in November, 1909 when members gave papers on 'Some Aspects in the Life of St. Paul'. Debate on topical issues was also encouraged with the subject of 'woman's suffrage' being debated in January, 1910. With declining membership and attendance at meetings the Guild at Hove closed in 2006 but the activities they embraced have continued in a different form. Both Dorset Gardens and Patcham have 'book clubs' whose members meet regularly to discuss novels. They each also have a bookstall. The devotional and educational activities could be said to have been subsumed in the 'House Groups' which exist in almost all Churches.

To some extent 'House Groups' have replaced both the Class Meeting, which has effectively disappeared, and meetings like the Guild. House Groups, which were introduced into the Brighton (Dome Mission) circuit by the Rev. Charles Banks (1981-1986), meet in members' homes and discuss a great variety of material about the faith including biblical studies. The discussion notes are sometimes provided by members and at other times nationally produced material is used. House Groups in Brighton and Hove have been meeting very successfully for many years and they have given those who attend them a deeper and fuller understanding of their faith.

Also mentioned earlier, music has been a basic part of Methodist life for a long time. Here we will look at music in Methodism other than that in worship. The prohibition on 'concerts' from the first decades of the nineteenth century was relaxed and through the century attitudes changed. There may have been three major factors for this. First, Sunday school Anniversaries needed entertainment and music was an obvious way of providing it and of getting the children involved. Secondly, events such as bazaars which became so much a part of church life, also needed some form of entertainment. Thirdly, offering entertainment was a way of getting people to come on to church premises.

When the Bible Christian minister the Rev. Jehu Martin arrived in Brighton in 1870 one of his first actions was to get 'public attention' and to introduce 'entertainments and other popular features'. The first recorded Wesleyan bazaar took place in 1885 to raise money for the new building at Dorset Gardens. Expenses for this bazaar, which took place in the grounds of the Pavilion, included moving a piano, and hiring a band and phonograph equipment. The Children's' Bazaar for the same purpose had taken place at Christmas 1884 and included a 'Sacred Cantata'. From this time onwards music both 'secular' and 'sacred' has been so much part of the 'Methodist diet' that many would be surprised to learn that at one time it was not so.

In the 1990s as part of the effort to raise money for the new Dorset Gardens Church, the Pastoral Assistant, Alan Cutting used his skills as a retired tourist advisor to organise a series of coach outings to places such as Stratford and Hampton Court. Even though the need for the money has largely disappeared such tours still take place and are an excellent way of providing both fellowship and entertainment.

There are also many activities and meetings for groups within the churches and most of them have meetings for groups such as: 'men', 'women', 'wives', 'the over-60s', many of whose members are not members of the Church. The work of just one group can stand for all. Hollingbury has always had the smallest membership in the circuit but the minute book of the 'women's club', which began in 1952 and lasted until 2006, shows much imagination and vigour in providing a great swathe of activities. These included: worship, fellowship, a programme of speakers at its regular afternoon meetings, a series of outings (in 1975 these ranged from Exbury Gardens in Hampshire to the Theatre Royal and the Brighton sewers!), refreshment, a crèche, 'sale of work', jumble sales, bazaars, social events, giving money to help a range of charities (in 1987 these included the RNID, the Mozambique Relief Fund, NCH Action for Children, Greenleaf, and Action for the Crippled Child), etc.

Although the 'chapel culture' of the late nineteenth century as a type of closed system has almost disappeared from the Methodist way of life, partly due to the fact that the state now provides so much, the Methodists of Brighton and Hove still provide a plethora of activities for members and non-members alike.

CHAPTER 12

The CHURCH in the WIDER SOCIETY

Methodism has always been involved in the life of the society in which it found itself. Although John Wesley instinctively supported the King and the 'powers that be' he encouraged his followers to vote and gave them advice on the matter. He also condemned activities like smuggling, expelling members who engaged in the practice. This approach to smuggling has been demonstrated by Rowland Swift in his study of Methodism in Sussex to have hindered the growth of Methodism in many parts of the county in the eighteenth century.

Wesley also had decided views on some of the major national and international issues of the day. He had strong, if somewhat ambivalent, views on the relations of Britain with her American colonies and was a strong, and non-ambivalent, opponent of slavery and the slave trade. Almost his last letter was to William Wilberforce encouraging him in the struggle against this trade.

At first both the Wesleyan and Primitive Methodists adopted a 'no politics' rule. By this was meant that partisan politics were not to be encouraged or adopted by Methodists. However there were certain political issues that affected Methodists. First, there were matters of direct concern. In 1811 the cabinet minister Viscount Sidmouth attempted to bring in a law that would have prevented any itinerant ministry. This would have destroyed Methodism. The Wesleyan Methodists organised a petition of over 30,000 signatures against this bill and raised money to support their campaign by collections in their societies. The Lewes and Brighton circuit raised over £15 in this cause of which Brighton contributed over one third. The overall result was not only a complete defeat for Sidmouth but also led directly to the Toleration Act of 1812, largely drawn up by Thomas Allan the connexional solicitor. This gave much greater freedom to those who were not members of the Church of England.

Secondly, there were general issues on which Methodists felt it their duty to become involved. They had always opposed both the slave trade and slavery itself. Methodists in Brighton must have heard of conditions in Barbados from the Rev. William Shrewsbury who had been forced to flee for his life in 1824 from that slave-owning colony and was stationed in Brighton for a year. In 1830 the Wesleyan Conference called for petitions against slavery and urged its members to consider that question as being paramount in the forthcoming general election. They eventually organised a petition with almost 230,000 signatures.

In Brighton this petition had a slightly unusual twist. During October 1830, the minister at the morning service at Dorset Gardens, the Rev. (Dr.) George Osborn, invited the congregation to sign the petition which was in the vestry. One member of the congregation, a visitor, came to the vestry and stated that he could not sign it but that he could present it to Parliament. He was the leading Whig M.P., Henry Brougham (the Whigs were the reforming party, later forming one tradition of what became the Liberal party). Consequently Brighton's petition was taken directly to Parliament by Brougham. The signing of petitions has continued to the present. Brighton and Hove Methodists were heavily involved in the petition for Jubilee 2000 organised by Christian Aid to cancel Third World Debt.

Much work remains to be done on the voting patterns of Brighton Methodists as revealed in the Poll Books for Sussex and Brighton before 1872. Brighton did not have a Member of Parliament until the 1832 Reform Act. All that can be stated at present is that those few Wesleyan Methodists who were qualified to vote for the two M.P.s for Sussex in the general election in 1820 all 'plumped' (that is they had two votes but only cast one vote as the other candidates were Tories) for Charles Cavendish, the defeated Whig candidate.

Brighton became a borough with an elected council in 1854. The first Methodist mayor was James Ireland in 1872, a member at Dorset Gardens, and from the 1880s there were a number of councillors and aldermen (who were councillors elected by their fellow-councillors to serve for six years. This office was abolished in 1971) who were members of one or other of the Methodist connexions.

In 1900 each of the connexions had members who were local councillors or aldermen, such as Cllr Henry Greenyer (Bristol Road Bible Christian Church), Alderman Edward Lowther (London Road Primitive Methodist Church), and Alderman John E. Stafford (Norfolk Road Wesleyan Methodist Church), who was Mayor of Brighton 1899-1902. Methodists have always regarded this kind of engagement with social and political issues as being a natural expression of their faith, the most recent Councillors being members of Hove Methodist Church, Alan Pratt (1995-1999) and Norman Wright (1992-1997).

The 'no-politics' idea of the first part of the nineteenth century gradually faded both as more people obtained the vote and as increasingly there were political issues, like 'free trade' and 'teetotalism', that aroused strong passions.

In Brighton and Hove the Bible Christians were especially vociferous in their temperance campaigning in the period between 1870 and 1910. In order to appreciate the reason for their passionate opposition to what they called the 'drink trade'. In his book, *Life in Brighton*, written in 1970 Musgrave noted that in 1860 there were in '479 liquor-shops compared with 541 provision-shops in the whole of the town.' and that it was also believed that 'the greater proportion of crimes committed in Great Britain was then attributable to drinking customs'. He commented specifically on the situation in Brighton that: 'Beyond all question the drink-shops contributed enormously to the poverty, degradation and misery upon which they flourished.'

It is in this context that we can appreciate the Rev. Jehu Martin's advocacy of temperance in all circumstances, a campaign that he took with him when he served on the Brighton 'Board of Guardians' which had responsibility for both the 'outdoor poor' and the workhouse. This involvement in local social questions has continued.

The Wesleyans were somewhat slower in adopting the cause of teetotalism. In 1873 the Norfolk Road trustees forbad their minister, the Rev. Hugh Price Hughes, from using their premises for a temperance meeting. However, this attitude changed and, as has already been mentioned, 'Bands of Hope' were a common feature of all Methodist connexions in the early part of the twentieth century. The emphasis changed from advocating total abstinence to responsible use.

It is symptomatic of the changing face of Methodism that there are now no 'Bands of Hope' attached to any Methodist church in Brighton, and it is instructive to read of the change of name in a committee. In 1925 at its first meeting the 'Brighton and Hove Temperance and Social Welfare Committee' only discussed 'temperance'. With one minor exception this single-mindedness continued until 1937 when other issues such as gambling were discussed. By 1950 the name had changed to the 'Circuit Christian Citizenship Committee' and by 1978 to the 'Circuit Social Responsibility Committee'. At the meeting in 1978 'temperance' was not mentioned at all, instead the committee received reports from the churches of the Brighton and Hove circuit on matters such as: 'the local community', 'hunger lunches', 'Methodist Relief Fund', 'Christian Aid', 'NCH' and 'world development'.

By the latter part of the nineteenth century there was a general identification of nonconformity with the Liberal Party. This was enhanced by the fact that the Liberal party was led for most of the century from 1868 by William Gladstone who, although a devout member of the 'High Church' wing of Church of England, appealed to Victorian nonconformity at its very deepest level. His speeches appealed to their consciences and his way of life was known to be devout. It so happened that the celebrations for the opening of Stanford Avenue Church in 1898 occurred at the same time as Gladstone was dying. This news evoked prayers for him. By the time of the first Sunday service it was known that he had died and the President of the Bible Christian Conference, who was leading the worship on that occasion, referred to Gladstone as one who was 'so eminent and so devoutly religious'. No other political leader has ever evoked such a response.

We have already seen how the political situation in Brighton was exacerbated by the strength of the Anglo-Catholic tradition and how in the General Election of 1900 the Conservative candidates in Brighton had no Liberal opponent, only the 'Independent Protestant', John Kensit.

In May 1902 the Conservative Prime Minister, Arthur Balfour brought in an Education Act that, in the words of Stephen Koss in his book *Nonconformity in Modern British Politics* 'unified and mobilised Free Church opinion as never before and never since'. One of the main features that provoked them was that they would have to contribute to Church of England schools through the rates which were paid by everyone regardless of church membership. The Conservative government further alienated nonconformist opinion by relaxing licensing regulations in the Licensing Act of 1904. Such was the feeling aroused by these measures that the Primitive Methodist Conference gave formal support to the Liberal Party.

In 1905 the final celebrations for the centenary of the first Wesleyan Class in Brighton were presided over by the Liberal M.P. for Scarborough, J. Compton Rickett, who was a prominent Congregationalist. In April of that year the sale of work at London Road Primitive Methodist Church was opened by one of the Liberal candidates for the forthcoming General Election, E. A. Ridsdale, whose principles were praised by the Superintendent minister as being those of the church. In the local elections of 1905 the Bible Christian Superintendent minister, the Rev. Samuel Brown Lane, who was a 'passionate Liberal', campaigned vigorously for the party which Funnell comments: 'many thought was one of the chief factors in the Liberal victory at that time.' The Liberals took both Brighton seats in the 1906 General Election, the only time that this was done in the twentieth century.

After World War I although Methodists in Brighton and Hove were always encouraged to vote and to use their vote wisely, explicit support for any particular candidate or party no longer occurred. The only exception was when, as the present writer recalls, the Rev. Frank Thewlis, Superintendent minister of the Brighton (Dome Mission) circuit, publicly supported the Labour candidate, Thomas Skeffington-Lodge who was a member of the Christian Socialist League, in the Brighton Pavilion by-election in 1969. It so happened that Skeffington-Lodge did not do very well.

From the 1960s until the late 1990s Dorset Gardens Methodist Church hosted the Labour Party Conference service whenever the Conference took place in the city. On one occasion this caused a furore. In 1966 an anti-Vietnam war demonstration took place during the service with protestors charging in followed by the media.

From the latter part of the nineteenth century, after Brighton had become a borough with its own council, Methodists were also increasingly involved in serving Brighton and Hove in other ways.

One example can stand for all of those whose faith has caused them to enter public service in one form or another. In 1888 Brighton appointed its first full-time Medical Officer of Health, Dr. (Sir) Arthur Newsholme. Newsholme was to remain at Brighton until 1908 when he was chosen as the

Medical Office of Health of the Local Government Board. He was a strong Wesleyan Methodist and a member at Dorset Gardens, holding several circuit offices including that of Circuit Steward. Both he and his wife were fully involved in the life of the Church and circuit. In his review of Eyler's recent authoritative study of Newsholme, Anthony Wohl commented that:

> 'No one contributed more in modern England, to the growth of preventative medicine and to the improvement of the quality of life for the working classes, or has received less recognition from historians for it, than Arthur Newsholme.'

In his conclusion Eyler commented that, 'at their core Newsholme's motives were moral' for he believed that human beings had a 'basic moral obligation … to one another' and campaigned, amongst other things to see that Brighton 'made provision to rehouse its poorest and least influential residents'. Newsholme created a Brighton Health Department that was called 'the model for other local authorities to emulate.' Eyler considers that it was his work in Brighton in 'constructing a comprehensive preventative strategy' to tackle tuberculosis that 'helped win him the Medical Officership of the Local Government Board'. Methodists like Newsholme made a positive contribution to the life of all who lived in Brighton and Hove.

The campaign regarding issues such housing did not end with Newsholme. In 1973 Hove Methodist Church took the lead in urging Hove Council to provide more public housing and in 1974 campaigned to increase the provision of hospital beds in Sussex for the elderly.

During both World Wars Methodists, as with all other Churches and countless other groups, tried to provide as much help as possible. The work of the Dome Mission at Dorset Gardens in World War II under its superintendent minister, the

Rev. George Simpson, was outstanding. To quote from Len Wright writing in 1985 of this period:

> 'Dorset Gardens [had a] ...Soldiers' Room for billiards and Rest Room, opened in 1940 ... and the Forces Friendly Hour after service on Sunday evenings. The Canteen was open every evening of the week from six to ten, run by a splendid and brave company of ladies ... Many of these ladies had well over a thousand hours to their credit. In one week prior to D-Day a thousand meals and cups of tea were served and in the year preceding VE Day, 20,000 meals ... were consumed. ... [at the] Thursday Family Evening ... church members and friends flocked to the premises and mingled with the service men so that all felt Dorset Gardens a veritable home from home.'

Methodists have always been concerned with 'mission'. At first it was thought of in terms of 'converting the heathen' both at home and abroad and in 1823 the Brighton Wesleyan circuit in 1823 had the July collection, 'to aid the spread of the Gospel in the unenlightened parts of Great Britain'. The Brighton branch of the Wesleyan Missionary Society was formed in 1815. All the Connexions supported and encouraged such work. Gradually the idea of 'spreading the Gospel' as a simple matter of 'converting the heathen' changed. Going to work alongside or help others became as or more important. Some members from Brighton and Hove, for example Grace Ovenden of Dorset Gardens, went to work in the 'mission field', in Grace's case as a teacher in Kenya. She was tragically killed in a car accident in 1955.

Clearly it would be impossible to mention all the activities in this area by the Methodists of Brighton and Hove over the past two centuries, so we will just refer to two of the most recent schemes which have focussed on assisting fellow-Christians in particular places. When the two circuits in Brighton and Hove united in 1997 it was decided to have a Circuit Project.

Under the leadership of the Rev. Doug Hopwood who already had a very good relationship with the then Anglican

Bishop of Jerusalem, the Rt. Rev. Riah Abu El-Assal, it was decided to form a partnership with the Arab Christian, Christ Church, in Nazareth. This was launched in March, 1999. The aim was to raise awareness of the situation of the small Christian community in the Holy Land, to increase understanding in both communities and to provide mutual support. Bishop Riah visited Brighton and Hove in 2004, addressed various Church and civic groups and received a cheque for £3,000 from the circuit. This visit was reciprocated later in the year by an official visit from the circuit, and in 2005 the new priest in charge of Christ Church, the Rev. Samuel Barhoum, came with his family to the circuit.

The Rev. Kathleen Allen, Circuit Superintendent minister, sharing greetings from the circuit with Christ Church, Nazareth, November, 2004

Below - Fr Samuel Barhoum, priest in charge at Christ Church, Nazareth, with his family at Stanford Avenue Methodist Church, August, 2005

In July 2001 the nineteenth World Methodist Council and Conference met in Brighton and Hove; following a suggestion by the Superintendent minister, the Rev. Mary Bailey, when she attended to Conference in Rio de Janeiro in 1996. One of the delegates in 2001 was the Rev. Jacob Freemantle from New Brighton, South Africa. In July, 2002 Dorset Gardens Church, under the leadership of Robin Dowsett and Nick Firrell, decided to create a partnership between the two churches similar to that of the Circuit Project and visits have been exchanged and mutual support, both spiritual and material, organised.

Most recently, in June, 2007, one of the most the most important features of this work was the visit, organised by the Rev. Cynthia Park of Dorset Gardens Church, of a choir from the Arthur Wellington Church, New Brighton, South Africa in the summer of 2007.

Choir from the Arthur Wellington Methodist Church, New Brighton, South Africa at Dorset Gardens Methodist Church, Brighton, 2007.

The Methodists of Brighton and Hove have not only been involved with work overseas. They have provided practical support for those in need: be it food for the unemployed in the 1920s and 1930s or hosting a 'soup run' for the homeless in the 1980s. These activities have always been seen as natural outworking of Wesley's idea of 'social holiness'.

In the twenty-first century the work goes on in a variety of forms. For example, on Wednesdays the Patcham Church organises a weekly lunch club for the lonely and elderly, and on Tuesdays and Thursdays organise a 'Mothers and Toddlers group'. Other churches serve in a similar way.

In 1998 Heather Leake (now Leake Date), a member at Stanford Avenue Church and a specialist pharmacist at the local NHS Trust, offered herself for the ministry. Since 1 September, 2002 she has been stationed in the circuit as what was formerly known as a 'Sector Minister' continuing her ministry in her secular job and establishing the role of HIV chaplain (and the Brighton and Hove Ecumenical HIV Chaplaincy). She is based at Dorset Gardens Church.

'Moved by the plight of children in Lambeth', the Wesleyan minister the Rev. Thomas Bowman Stephenson, with others, founded the National Children's Home (now NCH Action for Children) in 1869. Methodist have always supported this work, which they regard to some extent as, 'their charity', and have raised money and held meetings. For a number of years now Dick and Jean Morley have helped Methodists combine their love of 'tea' and their 'concern for others' by holding a circuit garden party in their large garden in Ditchling to raise money for NCH.

In these and countless other ways Methodists in Brighton and Hove have sought to put into action the words of Charles Wesley's hymn and have tried 'to serve the present age'.

CHAPTER 13

CONCLUSION

An attempt has been made in the preceding pages to give some idea of the life of Methodism in Brighton and Hove and its impact on the area over the past two hundred years. There have been many changes both in the city and in the church but the work and witness of the 'people called Methodist' continues albeit in ways that our forebears in the faith might find it difficult to recognise.

Methodism in Brighton and Hove had a most unusual origin in that it probably owed more to the arrival of the army in 1804 to repel any potential French invasion than to anything else. The Bible Christians, Primitive Methodists and United Methodist Free Churches all had their origins in a small group of lay folk inviting the relevant Connexion to send ministers to them.

Local Methodist practice has generally followed the national Methodist pattern, but occasionally there have been differences. The presence of George IV inadvertently led to Dorset Gardens having what may well have been the best orchestra leading worship in British Methodism for a while. The determination of the Rev. Frank Ballard in 1894 to continue his ministry for longer than maximum period of three years cannot but have had an effect on the campaign by the Rev. Hugh Price Hughes on this matter and on the whole 'Forward Movement'.

The 25-year ministry here of the Rev. William Dinnick was probably at the time of his death in 1901 the longest continuous pastorate in Methodism anywhere in the world, and his ability to get funding from devout members of the Church of England to build Primitive Methodist churches is also very unusual.

The Bible Christian tradition has been overwhelmingly rural. Clearly Brighton and Hove was unlike the small villages of Devon and Cornwall but from 1870 onwards in Brighton and Hove it became far more like the Wesleyan tradition and its role in Brighton and Hove is probably better understood in that light.

There has been a decline in the numbers of members but other evidence might well indicate that in some ways Methodism is as strong now in Brighton and Hove as it ever has been. It buildings and finances are in a good state, which is more than can said for much of the last two centuries. The numbers of house groups, prayer groups and study groups, together with developments in music and meditation indicate that the spiritual life of the circuit is still strong. It has certainly produced as many ministers in its last fifty years as in its first hundred and fifty. This is not to state that all is wonderful but it does mean that we need to take care in looking back at the past with too many rose-coloured spectacles. Some sociologists of religion like Grace Davie in books such as *Religion in Modern Europe: A Memory Mutates*, published in 2000, have argued that the current British religious context is one of 'believing without belonging' and it may well be that the Methodist concern with statistics may shield some important truths that we will need to tackle as the century unfolds.

Although any such history involves looking backwards the 'people called Methodists' have always been urged to look forwards and, to slightly misuse the phrase, say with John Wesley that 'the best is yet to be'. And so to finish with the same sentence with which the Rev. Ernest Griffin concluded his history 50 years ago. 'And so this story ends, but by no means is the story ended.'

printed in Great Britain by
One Digital
54 Hollingdean Road
Brighton, BN2 4AA